A Walk Across TEXAS

JON McCONAL

A Walk Across TEXAS

JON McCONAL

TCU PRESS • FORT WORTH, TEXAS

© 2008 Jon McConal
Library of Congress Cataloging-in-Publication Data

McConal, Jon, 1937-
A walk across Texas / by Jon McConal.
    p. cm.
  Includes bibliographical references.
  ISBN 978-0-87565-363-1 (alk. paper)
  1. Texas, West—Description and travel. 2. McConal, Jon, 1937—
Travel—Texas, West. 3. Lane, Eddie—Travel—Texas, West. 4. Hiking—
Texas, West. 5. Texas, West—Social life and customs. 6. Food habits—
Texas, West. 7. Texas, West—History, Local. 8. Historic sites—Texas,
West. 9. Texas, West—Biography—Anecdotes. 10. Interviews—Texas,
West. I. Title.
  F391.2.M245 2008
  917.6404'64—dc22

                                        2007028248

TCU Press
P. O. Box 298300
Fort Worth, TX 76129
817.257.7822
http://www.prs.tcu.edu

To order books: 800.826.8911

Cover photo courtesy of Pete Kendall, *Hood County News*.

In memory of Doug Clarke and Horace Chief Craig,

two men who were great editors and friends;

and to Phil Record, who taught me about

the power and beauty of writing.

TABLE OF CONTENTS

FOREWORD

Throughout his long career as a columnist and author, Jon McConal (his friends call him Bunky) has earned a position of trust among his readers. He has done this by listening to everyone he interviews as if they are disclosing to him the secrets of the universe, the meaning of life and death, and the formula for Coke. But they're telling him no such things. They're telling him something much more important to them. They're talking about themselves. All of us, I believe, in any age, want to be proud of who we are and what we have achieved. McConal patiently indulges this need in people. He's more than a writer. He's a doctor with the bedside manner of Dr. Kildare . . . uh oh, CODGER ALERT!

Oh, well. It's disclosure time. I'm an honorary member of Bunky's Camping Out and Codger's Club. I even went on one of his walks, a twenty-five mile trek from Weatherford to Mineral Wells. So, allow me to start over with another metaphor. Bunky is a literary photographer going down the road. He centers interesting people in his viewfinder and seldom, if ever, inserts himself into the picture.

He touts everybody he interviews because he chose them for a particular reason that was important to his story, and his instincts seem always to be right. A cherished eccentricity in their possession sometimes brings them together. It might be something he recognizes as iconic, a symbol, a precursor, or a rustic *objet d'art* held in esteem by its owner such as an old plow point that once turned dirt on a plow pushed by Bigfoot Wallace's nephew's best friend. It might be displayed over some proud owner's mantle. For the time it took to hear the story of the revered relic, Jon would take sincere, diligent, and prolific notes. During this ritual, the relic connects him, I believe, with its owners and previous owners and with history.

Again, most of us, sooner or later, learn the significance, and importance, of placing ourselves in a genealogical or historical context, at a location on a generational schematic in which we can pinpoint our unique place with our family. Rural people have always done this. Three or even four generations once lived together. Grandparents told the young ones stories of their ancestors and showed them fading photographs and other artifacts of the heart. The more people join the rush to suburbanize America, the more they alienate themselves from their past and a sense of community. It is fading fast. But it is still longed for.

And, this is where Jon McConal comes in. He places such store by these values that he is willing actually to put the boots on the ground, if I might appropriate that current political cliché. He goes into the Texas outlands and discovers this world that is now as foreign to most Americans as the Taj Mahal. But a literary photographer traveling down the road would never say such a thing. His job is to report, not opine. If Bunky has any such urges, he leaves them hanging in his Granbury closet.

In a moment of irony during the 450-mile walk across West Texas that is the subject of this book, Jon and his two walking companions, Eddie Lane and Norm Snyder, encounter a scene that Eddie describes as something to "really test your ability as a writer, Jon." But, again, this is what Jon does best. His eye goes as readily to outworn, abandoned remnants of another time and place as easily as the eye of the average member in good standing of the consumer generation might turn to the newest gadget that is at once a cellphone, a camera, a vibrator, a razor, and an automatic celebrity locator.

On they travel, into far West Texas and to Miami for information about the exciting cow-calling contest. In Miami he interviews a local denizen who avers that he'd rather dress up like a woman and get on stage than get in a cow-calling contest. In Turkey he and his companions visit the Bob Wills Museum, where in a display case they see a biography of Al Stricklin, the piano player in the band. The author? Jon McConal, of course. Then on to the West Texas towns of Matador, Dickens, and points west.

At this juncture I would like to honor Bunky's nose. I think he must have a nose like one of those water-dowsing rods. I have noticed that he is a master at capturing aromas that the rest of us miss, because if we go into the countryside at all we're probably inside a climate-controlled vehicle with the windows sealed shut. But his nose must be a marvel of a nose, a quick-salt nose, a nose finely tuned to prairie growth and wildlife and impending rain and livestock.

Near Breckenridge, on the way back home, he suddenly gets a snootful of his boyhood as the aroma of a corral wafts through the cedars. He leaves the road, ducks through the barbed wire fence, and there it is. It is blood he smells, from the corral. Somebody has been dehorning and castrating bulls, chores he did as a boy on his parents' ranches near Midland and Glen Rose.

He can distinguish between the various aromas of wildflowers, tree species, and even certain kinds of soil. Near Jayton he observes "the red clay banks of gullies eating into the canyon walls. Mesquite, schinery, and cedars covered the ragged steep sides of the canyon. The hillside had quilt-like coverings of prickly pear, juniper, and mustard grass with brilliant yellow blossoms. Huge clumps of Spanish daggers that looked like an old-time weapon of steel spikes grew in abundance."

They are interviewed several times on the trip, most notably by Bob Phillips, who asks Bunky what he has learned now that the trip is about over. Typically, he gives a nebulous answer. He's content to leave that part to the reader. Again, near the end of the walk they are sitting before their campfire in private contemplation of what they have accomplished. "No one said anything philosophical," Jon writes, almost as a point of pride, as if to say, "If it's Voltaire you want, read *Candide*." He doesn't inflict philosophy on the reader. It is the mystical, rather, that comes most naturally to him.

Going down the road, Trail Boss Bunky is all business. Philosophy detracts attention from the geography. And the country seems to be sinking under the weight of opinions. Opinions don't plant crops, irrigate the land, navigate the rivers and streams, repair the windmills and tractors, erect the oil and gas rigs, unclog the fences laden with tumbleweeds and in danger of ruin, or remove mesquite trees that are rampant now due to the eradication of the prairie dogs that lived off their roots. He is in tune with yearling cattle standing by abandoned farmhouses, and with the coyotes that "howl like wild women on the prowl," to quote one of his more mysterious similes. The research that precipitated such an image must have occurred before I made his acquaintance.

TOM DODGE

PREFACE

A distinct enjoyment to me is to travel by auto, canoe, or on foot down the many paths and rivers that cross Texas. The best way to discover these byways is by traveling across the state's roads and rivers that disappear over the horizon and leave civilization and its irritations behind. To hike in the footsteps of explorers, whether they were the Native Americans, Mexican traders, or French trappers, makes the journeys more interesting. Stories gathered from my travels with Jon McConal when put into print depict accurately what I experienced.

J. Frank Dobie in his book, *Tales of Old Texas,* said, "The way to spoil a story is to talk about it rather than tell it." McConal has the ability in his writing to tell the story and let others talk about his story-telling.

I continue to be astounded by the friendliness, kindness, and generous nature found in all of the people in West Texas. McConal expresses these feelings in his writing. As you read *A Walk Across Texas* you will sense a care and purpose in McConal's selection of words and thoughts that record his honesty and feelings for the roads, histories, and people of this area. From Perryton to Granbury, through the Panhandle and the plains of central Texas, you will read history of interesting people and places we encountered as we walked some 450 miles to visit with these people.

The people, places, and history we encountered in our travels from the Panhandle to the Gulf of Mexico have given me many pleasant memories. The roads of Texas present many stories waiting to be experienced and written about. I am certain when you have finished reading *A Walk Across Texas* you will say, "I wish I could have been with those three men."

McConal's ability to paint pictures of people and places is a rare trait for writers. When you read his description of a person and later meet this person, you will feel that you are already friends.

So take a seat in a comfortable chair and enjoy your walk across Texas. I know that I did.

EDDIE LANE

Chapter One

Three old codgers
Were feeling kind of rough
When one of them said
We need to show we're still tough.
We can sit here for months
Dwelling on all our complexes
Or we can get off our duffs
And do a walk across Texas.
Walk across Texas.
With its wonderful sights.
Walk across Texas.
With its beautiful nights.

Texas's majestic sites have always beckoned to me. I spent my childhood in the far regions of West Texas that have won a variety of descriptions, few of which are complimentary when it comes to commenting on the country-side. Those often sarcastic jibes never bothered me because I loved that area and its awesome sunrises and sunsets and the invigorating wild smells of the outdoors that reminded me of a person who has done a hard day's work and taken a bath using a thick bar of old time Lava soap to clean his skin and hidden crevices.

Another reason the arid desert landscape probably did not bother me lay in the fact that I frequently had my head buried inside a book. I learned how to read before the first grade and, as a result, I was one of the most frequent customers of the libraries in Kermit, Midland, and Odessa, towns in which I spent my childhood. I loved reading about people making long walks in Scotland and England. I can remember a book telling about the main character packing a backpack with the barest essentials and heading off for an extended adventure that would lead him through the countryside looking for the solution of some great problem.

Somewhere in that part of my life, I began thinking how great it would be to pack some meat and cheese and perhaps my mother's wonderful brownies and walk across Texas and experience some of its great adventures. I filed that idea in the back of my head for years. Then one day I mentioned it to Sharon Cox, who at that time was assistant state editor of the *Fort Worth Star-Telegram*. I expected that I would get the same negative response I had gotten before when asked if I had any great ideas for stories and I would say, "I think it would be neat to do a walk across Texas and write about the characters I will meet." Sharon, a person who seemed stuffed to overflowing with enthusiasm, surprised me when she said, "Write me an outline of where you want to walk and what kind of stories you think you will find." I did and two months later, my friend Doc Keen and I walked 350 miles across the western regions of the *Star-Telegram* circulation area. The response was so good that we made a second 350-mile stroll the next year.

After my retirement in 2000, I became friends with Eddie Lane of Granbury, who loves Texas and its outdoor delights as deeply as I do. We made a rather extended venture of following the Brazos River and looking at each one of the river's sixty-two bridges that resulted in my book, *Bridges Over the Brazos*. We told folks that we drove approximately 4,000 miles looking at the bridges. We were questioned about this since the river is only 900 miles long. Our standard answer to this question became "We got lost a lot." But, the real truth was, Eddie and I both indulged ourselves royally while looking at the bridges and deliberately took many wrong turns that we knew would not lead to a bridge but to some delightful spot of interest hidden along Texas backroads.

One night while we were camped at Washington-on-the-Brazos State Park, we had a good campfire going and we began talking about what our next adventure might be. Eddie had wanted to drive the roads that lead from El Paso along the Rio Grande to the Gulf Coast. That sounded fine. But, before the bridge trips were completed, the border became a rather hostile place with immigration and drug problems, not exactly the kind of place that two old codgers should be found camping. I kicked at the logs on the campfire and sparks flew into the air like a busted bottle rocket.

"Eddie, why don't we walk across Texas or at least a part of it? We could camp out along the way and I would write about the people we meet and work in some of the history of the area through which we are walking," I said.

Eddie got up and put another log on the fire. He looked at the stars smiling at us like a busted bucket of neon bulbs. "I think that would be a great idea," he said.

We went to TCU Press with the thought. They thought it was a novel idea and urged us to proceed. I thought that the fact that I am sixty-nine and Eddie is seventy-seven added to the interest of the book. In writing the manuscript, I would show people that there is no reason for people, regardless of their age, to sit on their duffs at home and become couch potatoes. They can and should get out and do something. I would augment that by writing something about myself that I seldom mention. I am an insulin-dependent diabetic and have been since I was twelve. Dealing with that has never held me back. During my professional writing career I made a fourteen-day canoe trip down the lower canyons of the Rio Grande. I have gotten up at midnight and driven two hundred miles to write news stories about a major airplane crash. I completed the two 350-mile walks. Eddie is another good example of not letting age or some of life's maladies keep you parked on an overstuffed easy chair. He has had one severe cardiac episode. Yet, he has canoed hundreds of miles on the Brazos and other Texas rivers. He has taken his grandson on an extended hiking and back-packing trip down the Grand Canyon.

Eddie's love of the outdoors came early in his life. He recalled being reared in Toledo. "I really didn't do any camping then. But, we went to vacant lots and played all kinds of sports, and just being outdoors became very special to me," he said. It was also in Toledo that Eddie developed a life-long love for fishing. He still has the first rod and reel and tackle box that he bought when he was eight years old. He used it for hours in a tiny pool called Heckie's Pond. "For bait we would walk in the shallow water for a few minutes. When we walked out there would always be a few small leeches attached to our legs. We'd pull those off and use them for bait," he said.

So began our plans for our great adventure. We considered several routes including following Interstate 20 from Fort Worth to El Paso. But, that route, as well as several others, would involve walking along highways that are thick with traffic. We studied our maps and finally decided on a route that would follow Highway 70 from north of Perryton in the Texas Panhandle south to Highway 180 and then back to our hometown of Granbury, a distance of 450 miles. We liked this route because the traffic is not particularly dense and the highways have well maintained shoulders on which we would be walking. Both of us are walkers, having about a three-mile-a-day average. So we knew that we would have to increase our mileage considerably to hit a fifteen-mile-per-day average that would lead us home in thirty days. Unfortunately, our training began in what became a record-setting heat wave that blistered our state. I admit that, during many of those days when the temperature boiled past 100, I wondered just what in the hell I was doing out walking an hour and a half in preparation for a 450-mile hike.

Some people offered discouraging remarks to us when they heard about what we were contemplating. But, we kept on training. We also began looking for a third person to go with us. We found that person almost by accident early one morning when Eddie and I were giving a speech about the book about the Brazos River bridges. During that pres-entation somebody asked us what our next project was going to be. We mentioned the walk and the fact that we were looking for a third person. Norm Snyder who was in the audience came up afterward and said, "I want to be that third person."

Snyder is sixty-two, an outdoor enthusiast and retired from IBM. He loves camping and wanted to increase his knowledge about Texas, where he has lived for the past twenty years. I had known Norm for several years. He and I attend the same church and for two years had worked together as volunteers in building houses in the Hood County Habitat for Humanity chapter. We both share some common interests and, since at the time, Eddie and I did not have a great number of volunteers for our third person, we made a quick decision. We immediately named Snyder a member of our expedition. Norm turned out to be much more than a driver . . . he walked the entire route after I suffered a back injury early on the walk, which caused us to change our plans considerably.

As the days drifted by and our training walks increased in mileage, I began researching other walkers. I read about a 400-pound man who was walking across America. He said he hoped he would not weigh 400 pounds when he completed his walk. I read about Dean Strickland, thirty-nine, a country singer who walks to his gigs, carrying his suitcase and guitar. He has found people to be very helpful. He has only been robbed twice. That reminded me of the two walks I made with Doc Keen. The only problem we faced on our treks came from an angry cousin of mine, who threatened me with bodily harm because I did not eat lunch with him and his family when we walked through their town. I told him that the town had 350 people who had attended a lunch in the city park, held especially for Doc and me. He still wanted to give me a thrashing.

I read about Grandma Gatewood in *The Whole Hikers Handbook*. Gatewood, after rearing eleven children decided she would start hiking. She did. When she was sixty-seven, she walked the entire Appalachian National Scenic Trail from Georgia to Maine. She became the first woman to walk the 2,000-mile course in one season. She didn't like expensive gear. She carried her few essentials, which included cheese, dried meat, bouillon cubes, powdered milk, raisins, nuts and crackers; a sweater, a jacket, a scarf, an army blanket to sleep in and a plastic curtain for shelter, inside a homemade denim bag with a single shoulder strap.

I read about the great John Muir who walked thousands of miles in our nation's wilderness areas, living like the animals for which he developed an intense love. He carried his entire backpacking gear in the pockets of an aging wool overcoat and when he became cold in the mountains, he found warmth by clearing a small space and then dancing all night to keep his blood flowing. And, there was John Wesley Powell, who lost his right arm during a battle in the Civil War, but led the first boating expedition down the Colorado and Green Rivers in the 1,000-mile run through the Grand Canyon. He became a folk hero, mapping the hostile land and chartering its wild rivers, sampling its archeological ruins, and unlocking its geologic mysteries.

Then there are the countless stories of our pioneering forefathers and mothers. They came to the West in wagons packed with their belongings and families. Often because of a lack of space in the wagons, family members trudged behind them, wearing old brogans that had been split repeatedly from the rocks and ragged escarpments over which they walked. Those people averaged ten miles a day, so historians say.

So when looking at all of those stories, I figured, why couldn't three old codgers like Eddie, Norm, and me walk at least fifteen miles a day? A final argument in favor of the walk came from the knowledge of my two previous walks. I knew that when you get close to the people and to the country by actually walking across the land, you make discoveries that are hidden from those who speed across the land in motorized vehicles.

We saw some of this when the three of us drove our route in August. The country then still lay browned and burned by the recent drought that had clamped hard on nature with its dry jaws. But, as we drove, I saw things that I knew we would enjoy looking at and observing more closely. Places like the washing machine museum in Mineral Wells and the old county courthouse in Palo Pinto. Stories from the past echo vibrantly in these structures. Like I always can hear the booming voice of the late Sam Cleveland when I drive past the Palo Pinto courthouse. I covered several trials that Cleveland, known as Mister Sam, prosecuted and always felt relief that I never had been subjected to his commanding cross-examination on the witness stand.

We drove through Stephens County where the odor of a recent pasture fire still hung heavily in the air. We saw the marks from the fire that had scorched trees and left long streaks of black on the countryside like an old pair of black shoes that had been poorly polished. We looked at the lingering eyes of coals in some of the tree stumps. During a stop for a drink of water, Norm talked about his background. He served in the air force twelve years and worked around the world in radar maintenance. He spent his childhood in West Virginia. The family property bordered a forest.

"When I got out of school each day, guess where I disappeared to?" he asked with a faraway look in his eyes. He also told us about his love of skydiving and SCUBA diving. "When I was a small boy, probably in the fifth grade, I decided that I would become a skydiver and a SCUBA diver. The small town where I grew up had an army/navy surplus store where I found a parachute. I bought it and took it home. My father immediately made me cut the lines off of the canopy. He quite correctly deduced that I planned to jump off of something. I hadn't formed an exact plan at that point in time, but that was exactly what I had in mind."

He smiled. "Since there isn't much clear water in West Virginia, SCUBA is not common and both ambitions went on the back burner. I spent a lot of time with my scout troop. And, that led to another interest," he said. That interest was sailing, which came as a result of Norm's pragmatic, engineering mind. He devised a way that two seventeen-foot aluminum canoes could be lashed together with six feet of freeboard between. Part of his parachute canopy became the sail. "We had a canoe catamaran," he said. I could just imagine the wild adventures Norm and his buddies must have had.

We continued west through rugged pastureland with cattle trying to find grass as they grazed with their heads looking like they were attached to the ground. We drove through oil country and saw several antique drilling rigs that had been dragged to the pasture and left for nature to take care of. One looked like some aging monster from outer space, with all of its wires and cables and rusting steel girders. Cattle stood in a nearby grove of mesquites, switching their tails slowly at flies landing on their sides and backs.

We reached the country known as West Texas and saw huge clumps of tumbleweeds or Russian thistles. I remembered having to cut these weeds from fencerows when I was a youngster living in Midland. Leave them alone and maybe in two years you wouldn't have a fence because the weeds trapped the sand that blew in that area and soon the fence would be totally covered.

We pushed on through Dickens County where we saw a flock of wild turkeys eating grasshoppers beside the roadside. The birds suddenly burst into flight and barely sailed over the car.

We crossed the Red River, a stream that flows in a color like its name, looking like somebody had spilled a giant bucket of blood from a slaughter-house. Back in the distance we saw something we had not seen for months in our country, rain clouds. We kept driving and ahead of us a giant blue sheet appeared as rain emptied from the sky.

We drove through Perryton and reached the Oklahoma border and we stopped at Mike's Red Barn that had brightly painted signs advertising beef jerky and ice cold beer. We climbed from the car to stretch our legs. Several trucks were parked in spaces around Mike's and another business across the road.

"Norm, we are only forty miles from Liberal, Kansas," said Eddie.

"Damn," said Norm. "And this is where the walk is going to start? Damn." He answered his own question.

We wanted to get a picture. I walked to a pickup and asked the driver if he would mind taking our picture.

"No, I'll be glad to," he said. Eddie explained the workings of his camera and the three of us stood together.

"What's this for?" asked the man, built solid and wearing suspenders.

"Oh, we are going to make a 450-mile walk from here," said Eddie.

(Left to right) Norm Snyder, Jon McConal, and Eddie Lane stand at the Texas state line eight miles north of Perryton where the 450-mile walk began. Photos by Eddie Lane and Norm Snyder.

"Four hundred and fifty miles. My gawd, boys, why are you gonna do that for?" asked the man.

"We just thought it would be neat to say that we walked that far," said Eddie.

The man snapped the picture and handed the camera back to Eddie.

"I ain't never heard of such a thang," he said. He looked at us. "One time, I drove all the way from Oklahoma to California without stopping, except for gas and to take a couple of pisses. But, walk 450 miles, I never even dreamed of something like that. But, well, it sounds like a good idea, I guess. Regardless, let me wish you luck. And, if you get real thirsty, well, drink a Lone Star, if you can find one. They will satisfy your thirst. Four hundred and fifty miles. Wait until I tell Mildred this. She won't believe me."

We thanked him. I walked over to the side of the road and gazed down it, thinking about what we were going to do. My mind wandered and suddenly I got the idea about writing a song about our walk and beginning each chapter with a verse or two. I jotted a note about that and decided that the best time to write the song would come on the walk. That's how the song *A Walk Across Texas* came about.

I made one final look at what would be our start on October 3, 2006. I could hardly wait for the adventure to begin.

Chapter Two

So they drove north
To where Oklahoma begins
Then they began walking
Through those fierce Texas winds.
Walk Across Texas
With its wonderful sights.
Walk Across Texas
With its beautiful nights.

Our departure looked like a family reunion. We met at the Lane's house with our wives. Jane and I also took our dog, Cleo. Eddie and Jane's dog Mattie joined the entourage outside as we laid all of our gear near the tent trailer that would be our home for the next month. Eddie was more proud of the trailer than Norm and I. He should have been. He only paid $300 for it. It looked like it. We soon named it our Highway Hilton.

As we packed our gear into the trailer and car, Cleo and Mattie looked like they were about to lose their best friends. Our wives laughed and joked.

"Don't forget where you live," said Barbara Snyder.

"We won't," said Eddie. "And, you girls behave yourselves. We'll see you in a month or two."

We gave last minute hugs and then we were off. Cleo looked out of our auto and barked. I knew I would miss her almost as much as Jane. Still the thought of whether this was such a great idea tugged at me. I realized it was a little too late to back out now. We decided that we would go a shorter way to reach the start of the trip so we headed north on Highway 4 to Highway 281.

We reached Windthorst about eleven A.M. and stopped at the Windthorst General Store, which is always a traveler's treat. I remembered my first stop there more than forty years ago after I had gone to work at the *Fort Worth Star-Telegram* as a ranch and farm writer. It was a delight then and time certainly has not changed it.

You can buy a mean German sausage sandwich there as well as hamburgers and burritos. You can also buy things like lariat ropes from a wide selection of ranch supplies. I wandered across the creaking wooden floors looking at straw hats, walking shoes, boots and riding gear. After a half hour of looking, we continued north to Archer City, home of author Larry McMurtry who has written many best sellers including *Lonesome Dove* and *The Last Picture Show*, from which hit movies were made. We wanted to stop at his well-stocked bookstore but it was closed so we headed on north.

We drove past pastures full of mesquite and I remembered reading in the *Texas Almanac* about that thriving tree. The almanac states there are more than 200 varieties of mesquite, the honey variety being the one that dominates Texas pasturelands. Ranchers spend thousands of dollars fighting mesquite. Before it became such a problem Mother Nature curtailed mesquites with pasture fires and the ubiquitous prairie dog, which loved to chew through its root system and eat the wood. Ranchers controlled the grass fires and killed the prairie dog by feeding them poisoned grain. No more grass fires and no more prairie dogs. Instead, there are millions of mesquites that require a constant battle to control.

As Eddie drove a thought that had been heavy in my mind during all of our planning came back: Would the three of us be able to get along without any major conflicts during a month of what was going to be fairly intense association? I knew that Eddie and I had managed without any problem when we had done the research for the bridges book. We had camped out for a week at a time on two different occasions and had not had any major argument. I think one thing that prevented this was an agreement we had made early on that we would not discuss politics or religion at any time. When we talked to Norm about making the trip, we emphasized this point and he agreed that it was a good idea.

We passed freshly plowed and planted grain fields. Tiny stems punched through the reddish colored dirt as a result of recent rains. I looked at the new growth and thought of the sad news I had gotten the day before we left about the death of Horace "Chief" Craig, a longtime and dear friend and former city editor at the *Fort Worth Star-Telegram*. Chief, as all of his friends called him, had taught me so much about writing. He was a huge man with large, strong fingers that had such a gentle touch when it came to editing stories young writers like me had created. He made them sound much better than they had been written. Aw, gosh, I would miss him.

We drove past oil field pumps running slowly in their up and down movements as they dragged the oil from the bowels of geological formations. We drove over the Wichita River and through Electra and Childress where gas was advertised for $1.99. We passed a hamburger café that had a steel cutout of a standing man firing a rifle. Close by stood the Turtle Hole Car Wash and a church sign that read, "You can't control the winds. Adjust the sails."

We crossed the Red River and its big wide channel with clay banks colored red like the face of a woman with too much make-up. We stopped at Vernon and ate lunch at Roma's Italian Restaurant. Norm was amazed that we found such good Italian food in a town like Vernon. We also discovered that the tread from one of the tires on the Highway Hilton had torn loose. We went to a Wal-Mart and bought two new tires, had them installed and pushed onward.

I asked Eddie to play a compact disc that had been given to me by my longtime, late friend Doug Clarke. (Clarke died in January 2007, shortly after I had finished writing this manuscript.) Clarke claimed he had directed the effort that was produced by his son Zach. He called it "McConal's Magnificent Walking Tour Symphony." It had twenty songs, including "I Walk the Line," "Move it On Over," "Walk, Don't Run," "The Magnificent Seven," and "I Ran All the Way Home." Clarke had also written some advice for me. It read:

> "In honor of Jon McConal's third Texas Walking Tour in which he has finally figured out it is better to walk in a straight line than go in circles, this record has been produced to highlight the new paradigm McConal has discovered in walking in a straight line. Each song was individually tested and selected and listened to, to increase the thirst and desire for cool beverages such as Johnnie Walker Black, Black Jack Daniel, or Cutty Sark. The genre of music selected encompasses all styles of getting on with it. The compilation comprises the music me and Bunky [a nickname to which many of my friends refer to me] have listened to and enjoyed. Walk with care."

The three of us kept time to the music and I sang along with some of them. Norm smiled and said, "That was a helluva nice thing for your friend to do. I'd like to meet him someday."

We drove past fields of cotton that looked like they had been dusted with snow and were ready for picking. We passed bois d'arc trees with piles of their tough apples lying on the ground.

"Those are Aggie oranges," said Eddie.

"We call them Osage oranges in West Virginia," said Norm.

We drove through Shamrock and across some remains of old Route 66, that 2400-mile highway that carried thousands from the Dust Bowl scarred lands of the southwest to California and a hope of finding jobs and a better life. South of Canadian, Norm spotted a large dinosaur made out of steel and perched on a hill. The sculpture just stood there like it was gazing at all of the crazy motorists speeding by below it.

We arrived at Wolfcreek Park near Perryton at 5:50 P.M. We picked out a camping site that would be our home for the next five days and began unloading. Norm and Eddie would sleep in tents. I was assigned to the Highway Hilton with its series of sways and moans when I moved about on my air mattress. Each night turned into a challenge of whether I could turn over without rolling off the sheet of plywood holding my mattress pad.

Eddie cooked a dinner of smothered steak, potatoes, onions, and peppers. I sipped my drink and talked to him while he cooked. He had planned extensively for our meals and explained his reasoning. "I figure that our walking pace is going to be about twenty-two minutes per mile. We will be burning about sixty-five calories per mile. That will push our calorie consumption to about 2,700 calories a day, if we maintain our pace," he said. "That's why for every meal we need a meat, like steak, pork chops, or chicken and a good carbohydrate like potatoes or beans. We also will need some fresh vegetables that we will get with our salads. And, of course I've brought plenty of fresh fruit."

I stepped back and smelled the food. It had a wonderful odor as it simmered in the huge iron skillet. I learned that it would be typical of the meals Eddie would cook throughout the rest of the trip. On this night, we added large spoonfuls of salsa. The concoction tasted delicious. We finished and sat in chairs around our campground. Nobody said anything deeply philosophical. We listened to some country music and climbed into our beds at ten P.M.

"We are three really active men," said Eddie.

With my alarm set for one-thirty A.M., I planned to get up and check my blood sugar. I like to have a reading between 65 and 185; much too wide a range says my doctor. But, it seems to have done me well. My reading was eighty-five this night. I ate some honey to raise my blood sugar. I climbed out of the Highway Hilton and looked at the stars. They were beautiful; like somebody had thrown a bucket of lighted glass into the sky. Again, I began thinking about this whole idea. Is it really a good thing? Will we be able to complete it?

I looked up at the Big Dipper. I thought of the coming walk again and imagined taking a drink from that star formation when I became thirsty. I crawled back inside the Highway Hilton. I listened to the night sounds that included a symphony from insects and birds. I thought of Jane and Cleo. Gosh, a month seemed like a long time. I finally went to sleep.

Chapter Three

We camped near Perryton
We heard the coyotes howl.
They made quite a symphony
Like wild women on the prowl.
Walk across Texas
With its wonderful sights.
Walk across Texas
With its beautiful nights.

Two owls talking to each other woke me up on our first day to walk. I lay there and listened to them and wondered if they were the same ones I had listened to last night. I finally unzipped my sleeping bag and walked outside. A fifty-nine-degree temperature greeted me. The smells of coffee brewing came strongly from the camp stove. Strong windblasts rattled the sides of the Highway Hilton and the tree limbs.

We ate and headed for the Oklahoma border, driving through Perryton with its wide streets and then through nine miles of farmlands. Gigantic tractors with equipment attached to them sat near barns, awaiting their owners and long hours in the fields.

Norm looked at the land and sighed. "I don't think this is going to be one of our most scenic days," he said.

Eddied laughed and said, "This will really test your ability as a writer, Jon."

We reached the Oklahoma state line and stopped near the Chavas Bar. A man unloaded beer from his truck and pushed the cases inside. Somebody was going to have fun that night. Eddie and I tightened our shoelaces, said goodbye to Norm and began walking the first steps of our big adventure.

The wind had picked up and we were walking right into it. Eddie figured it must have been hitting twenty miles an hour. That, plus the powerful gusts created when large trailer trucks roared by sent our hats spinning to the bar ditches frequently. We kept walking. About two miles after we started we saw our first dead rattlesnake. It had been run over by a car.

After an hour we stopped at an abandoned farmhouse for our first break. A windmill without any blades stood in the backyard. I remembered my childhood days in Midland, Texas, when we lived on a ranch and had a windmill in our backyard. One of my favorite things to do after awakening in the morning was to run to the windmill, put a tin cup beneath its faucet and fill it with the cold water being pumped from 300 feet in the ground. Gosh how great that water had tasted. One morning I put the cup to my mouth without looking and started to take my drink when I realized that a tarantula had crawled into the cup overnight and had sat there when I filled the cup with water. When I raised it to my mouth, the tarantula simply clamped itself to my nose and mouth. I quickly swiped it away and took off running. I don't think I stopped for a mile. My brother, who had watched the incident, said I probably set a record in the mile run.

I took a drink from my bottle of water that I carried in my fanny pack. It tasted good but not like the taste of that cold well water in West Texas. I walked over to the house that had paint peeling from its window frames with broken glass panes. I looked at a huge tree in the backyard and thought how many hours children must have spent climbing and tying ropes to its limbs to fashion swings. Many of the massive limbs had died and looked like dried twisted chunks of leather. Some yearling cattle stood nearby swatting flies with their tails and licking their lips as they looked at me like I was supposed to be bringing them feed. I took one last look and joined Eddie to continue our walk.

About a mile from Perryton Norm greeted us. "Boy have I struck a gold mine for you, Jon. I stopped at the Museum of the Plains in Perryton and met some people who have lived here forever. They want to meet us and want to take us to the Lions Club luncheon," he said.

We drove to the museum and met Dempsey Malaney and Norman Allen. Malaney, a large, strong-looking man with his hair combed straight back, said he represented the fourth generation of his family living on the ranch where he and his wife, Kara, resided. He led us through the museum and stopped at a photograph of an elderly woman smoking a pipe.

"That's my great-grandmother, Mary Octavia Jackson," he said. "Her husband was a buffalo hunter and yes sir, we are still on the same place that they settled. Her husband was Ben Jackson and after all the buffalo were killed he became a freighter. They came here from Dodge City, Kansas, and wait until you see the stove and pump organ that he hauled in here for Grandma. We still have a hand dug well that is lined with rock that we get water from and water our garden. Yes sir, you boys are in for a treat when I take you out there and it's right on past where you are camped."

We finished our look at the museum and then Malaney drove us to the local country club and the Lions Club luncheon. We were greeted warmly but many people could not believe we were on a 450-mile walk. One member shook his head and asked, "You folks have cars down in Granbury?"

Russell McElroy, high school girls volleyball coach, spoke after the meal, telling about the power of the local team and how far he expected them to go in this year's competition. He said he had graduated from

Perryton High School and had made first team all-district defensive end in football.

"Coaching girls volleyball is just putting into it and other sports the feeling and competition that is in football . . . you got to transform that feeling into all sports and yes, I certainly am enjoying trying," he said.

Eddie listened and then asked if the wind ever stopped blowing in this part of the country. "Stop," one of the members said. "It hasn't even started."

We returned to the museum where we met Terri Suitor, the director, and James Coverdale, a wall of a man and a Kiowa Indian. He showed us a teepee that he had helped build and put up that had some intricate Kiowa designs he had fashioned. He said his great-great grandfather was known as Two Hatchets.

"He got that name after he had been on a raid into Central Texas. He was walking away from a cabin and saw these two hatchets sticking into a log, so he pulled them out and brought them home with him. He said they were the trophies from his raid and as a result acquired the name Two Hatchets," said Coverdale.

He said Two Hatchets became a chief of the Kiowas and fought at Adobe Walls, a famed battle in the Texas Panhandle where some twenty-two buffalo hunters fought several hundred Indian warriors to a standstill. Two Hatchets may have even been responsible for the battle at Adobe Walls, a small community created to serve buffalo hunters and skinners. The settlement lasted only a few months during the last days of buffalo hunting.

"About a week before the battle, Two Hatchets and some more Kiowas killed two buffalo hunters by cutting off their hands, cutting open their stomachs and then driving a stake through their intestines," he said. "Brutal . . . yes. But that was the Indian way."

One of those men had been John Thomson Jones, alias "Antelope Jack" or "Cheyenne Jack," a buffalo skinner. An old photograph shows him to be a short, lean man. He is wearing a cartridge belt, and a huge skinning knife hangs from it. After the bodies of Thomson and his friends were found, about 200 Comanche, Kiowa, Cheyenne, and Arapaho Indians attacked Adobe Walls on June 27, 1874. The Indians had been told by their medicine men that they would be able to club to death the men at Adobe Walls while they slept. And even if they awoke, the medicine men said the white men's bullets would pass through them without causing any harm.

But, as the Indians climbed onto the roofs of the two stores, the buffalo hunters began shooting through the ceiling of the buildings, killing some thirteen Indians. The warriors retreated to some nearby hills for a conference. The conference ended quickly when one of the buffalo hunters stuck his rifle through a window, aimed and shot; killing one of the Indians from a distance of what some historians claim was a mile. Regardless, the Indians had had enough and left this tiny trading post that eventually was abandoned. I had visited the site that is halfway between Spearman and Stinnett in Hutchinson County on an earlier journey. Because of time, we were not able to drive there during our walk.

We finished our visit at the museum and followed Malaney to the outskirts of town to begin our walk. He warned us about walking up Apple Hill. "That's where the folks used to take a car they were considering buying. If it could make it up Apple Hill then they knew it was all right," he said. "So you boys be sure and watch Apple Hill. And, why don't I come and pick you up about four P.M. and show you our ranch."

We shook hands and said that would be an excellent idea. Then we began the second half of our fifteen-mile walk that day. And, yes, Apple Hill did prove to be a rather tortuous climb. But, we finished it and returned to camp. After a short rest, Malaney arrived to give us a tour. He sounded like a verbal history book as he pointed out sites where things had happened in the past century and a half.

"That old tree to the left is called the Witness Tree," he said pointing to a huge tree with twisting dead limbs. "Surveyors used it in surveys and all people coming through here then used it as a landmark. Now this is our ranch. Right over there on that creek is where my great-great grandfather let the Kiowas camp."

We reached the house where he and his wife Kara live. A flock of wild turkeys strutted across the front yard. He led us inside and introduced us to Kara and then showed us the majestic wood stove that his great-great grandfather had hauled in from Dodge City.

"I've eaten some good meals cooked on that stove by my aunt," he said. "My great-great grandmother touched the side of the stove one day when it was hot. She fell backwards and broke her hip and never recovered."

We looked at the old pump organ his great-great grandfather had hauled here on a wagon. Then we walked outside and looked at the well, hand dug in 1911 and lined with rock that had been cut from the countryside. He lowered a bucket attached to a pulley that made a howling, squeaking noise. We heard it hit the water. Malaney pulled it to the top and urged us to put our hands inside the water. We did. It was ice cold.

"We don't drink it any more but I use it to water my garden," he said.

He drove us around the ranch some more, explaining the importance of various trees, piles of rocks, and other things. I asked him why preserving this history was so important to him.

"It honors our great-grandparents and grandparents and makes us understand all they went through to make it in this country back then. I credit my junior high school teacher Spencer Whippo with firing my interest in history. He was a hands-on type who took us kids out to various historical sites and explained what happened. But, history, oh yeah, it is so important," he said.

He drove us back to our camp site and said he would meet us again tomorrow afternoon to look at another very important local historic site where what is called the buried city had been located. He said he would bring some experts with him to explain what has been called one of the most important finds in Texas.

After he left we all poured ourselves a drink and watched as the sun set and blistered the western sky in a stunning array of red, orange and black colors. Norm watched and said, "I think I am going to like this trip."

After dinner, we listened to the radio for about an hour. Then we said goodnight and headed for our beds. I crawled into the Highway Hilton and sank onto the air mattress. I listened to the night sounds that included a repeat high volume verse from a bank of crickets. They had reached their third verse when I slipped into a deep sleep.

Chapter Four

We walked past cattle
Fat as big whales
They stared at us
And, swatted flies with their tails.
Walk across Texas
With its wonderful sights.
Walk across Texas
With its beautiful nights.

Coyotes woke me up singing a wild symphony about a mile off in some pastureland. I lay there and listened and then kicked my sleeping bag off and crawled out of the Highway Hilton. Eddie had the coffee started and it smelled delicious.

We drank coffee and talked about our coming day. Sharon Ellzey, owner of KEYE, the radio station in Perryton, had requested that we come and be on the early coffee hour program that she hosted each day. "I'll give you all of the coffee you want plus I promise you will have a good time," she said. "You are bound to be a hit. My gosh, three guys your age doing something like this. Hey the listeners are bound to find this interesting."

"We may become the next Edward R. Murrow," said Eddie as we loaded up and headed for town. Sharon greeted us warmly. She's a pretty woman with rust colored hair cut short. She is energetic and enthusiastic. We talked for a half hour, telling why we were taking a walk across Texas and why we felt anyone could do the same kind of thing if they just set their mind to it.

After the show ended I visited for a few minutes with Bob Byer, the general manager. He is a retired marine and worked as a combat correspondent dealing with newspapers and broadcast media during his career. When he retired he heard about the job here in Perryton. He called and they said they needed someone with experience like his, someone they could trust. He gave them his background and he was hired.

"I lived in a small town in Wisconsin. As a matter-of-fact there were only twenty-seven in my graduating class. So I took the job, and yes, we like it here," he said.

We drove back to where we had quit walking the day before and began our daily trek through Ochiltree County, which borders Oklahoma, and is in the Texas High Plains, located 120 miles northeast of Amarillo. We had passed from farming land and had reached the ranching country. The county spreads over 907 square miles of level prairies that are sliced through by Wolf Creek, South Wolf Creek, Palo Duro Creek, and Chiquita Creek. Native grasses and wheat, grain sorghum, corn, and alfalfa all grow on the clay and loam soils. The economy is helped by oil and gas production.

Irrigation aided the crop production and the Perryton Chamber of Commerce said that led to the title, "Wheatheart of the Nation" when the county became the leading wheat producer in the nation. The chamber also notes that Perryton won the Texas Hardworking Rural Community award from the Texas Department of Agriculture in 2003 and the city's Wright Elementary School won the 2004 Blue Ribbon No Child Left Behind award.

As I gazed south at the distance that we were to cover, the immense nature of our task dawned on me. I knew we could do it, but I wondered what I would be thinking in two weeks when I looked south and realized that we still had two more weeks to go. I shook my head and laughed at myself. Here we were only on the second day of walking and already I was wondering if this was such a good idea.

We passed the site of Ochiltree, the first seat of the county and once a town of 500 people. Today the location has a cemetery and a few old ruins. I recalled reading an unusual thing about the town in Dr. T. Lindsay Baker's book, *More Ghost Towns of Texas*. He said that a popular activity at Ochiltree was automobile racing. In 1915 a track was built around a natural playa lake and local promoters advertised a coming race with $2,000 in prize money.

"Entrants began arriving two and three days early, coming in cars from such manufacturers as Buick, Hudson, Stutz, and Pierce-Arrow. The first prize of $760 went to Charles and John Ensminger in a Hudson Super Six," wrote Baker. "The promoters realized a profit and set up additional races, primarily to boost the image of Ochiltree in the surrounding country and also to bring visitors to the town."

But when the railroad bypassed the town in 1919 and 1920, the sounds of racing cars and other activity almost ceased. Perryton was established eight miles north and a big move started from Ochiltree. As Baker said, "Many of the residences and commercial buildings, which were of wood frame construction, were transported from the banks of Wolf Creek across the flat plains to the new railroad town. Ochiltree became a ghost town in just a few months. The county seat moved to Perryton in 1919 and in 1921 the post office was also transferred."

Bye, Bye Ochiltree. Today, only echoes of the stiff wind from the north whipped through the site. Well, there still were lots of wildlife as evidenced by the two carcasses of red tail fox and two bodies of rattlesnakes we passed. Also, we passed a feedlot but the stiff north wind kept the smell behind us.

James Coverdale, dressed in his Kiowa Indian tribe clothing, talks with Eddie Lane and Jon McConal, left, and Norm Snyder, right. Photos by Eddie Lane and Norm Snyder.

I had not told anybody about a growing concern of mine. I had obviously strained my back while unloading some of our gear and my back felt like it had a live coal in the lower right side. I had decided to keep on walking and not say anything. But, after today's walking, I wondered how much longer I could go on.

We took a break and ate lunch. We walked three more miles and then returned to our campsite. We had been promised a visit to the buried city, an important pre-Columbian site on Wolf Creek eighteen miles southeast of Perryton at three P.M. that afternoon. We drove there and met Scott Brosowske, a research archeologist for Harold Courson and his son, Kirk, who own the land. James Coverdale, dressed in Kiowa clothing, also was present. He wore a headdress or war bonnet, a feathered flag and other regalia that he called Kiowa Sunday go-to-meeting clothes.

The site became well known to buffalo hunters and early ranchers in the area by the late 1870s because of its impressive ruins visible above the ground. Brosowske, a graduate of the University of Texas at Austin, told about being hired by the Coursons who had recognized the historical importance of the area and had purchased the land.

"Actually, teams came out in 1907 and began digging here. It was the first archeological excavation ever done in the state of Texas," he said.

Before that, local people had found the mounds and site fascinating. So fascinating that they would drop a quarter in a coffee can at the gate of the ranch to come in and look for arrowheads and other items. They found an abundance of those plus pottery pieces and animal and human bones that they took home with them. An archaeologist who came to the scene in the early 1900s was Warren Moorehead of Andover, Massachusetts. He said the ancient village site extended over 3,000 feet along Wolf Creek and was the product of a fairly advanced aboriginal culture of unknown origins.

Courson, former Perryton mayor and president of Courson Oil and Natural Gas Association, recognized the importance of the site and purchased it and surrounding property. Then through his efforts, the Texas Historical Commission was given two easements of about fifty acres and the site was listed in the National Register of Historic Places. Thank goodness for people like the Coursons.

Before we drove to the site, Brosowske showed us items that had been found during exploration of the land. They included a steel picket used to drive into the ground and hold horses, a steel iron once used to press clothing that had the handle cut off and used as an anvil by Indians, a Mexican horse bit and a piece of an old spur.

Then we loaded ourselves into pickups and drove to the site of the buried city. We passed a flock of wild turkeys and saw two mule deer. Brosowske pulled over and we crawled out and listened as he gave information about the site.

"The inhabitants apparently left about 1400, about a hundred years before Coronado came through here," he said. "Many people think it was a drought that drove them away but I think it was probably something else though I am not certain what it was."

He said the first people who looked at the region found areas with little mounds of rocks laid out in squares and rectangles. Some of those first observers thought that the people who lived here were mound builders. But, later excavations proved that the squares and rectangles had been houses. Many were built on a scale that was massive by prehistoric standards. One house was found to have more than 650 square feet of floor space, a hearth, and wooden posts up to eighteen inches in diameter that formed roof supports.

"If you look across the field you can see darker circles in the grass. Those are where excavations have been done," said Brosowske. He pointed and we could see the darker mounds. By letting your mind wander and using a bit of imagination you could sense the settlement that once stood here, smell the fires cooking corn and meat and hear the voices of small children running through the native grasses. One bit of information I had found on the Internet called the buried city site one of the most important and fascinating archeological finds that sheds light on the fascinating and historic past of the Panhandle (http://www.texasbeyondhistory.net).

After about an hour and half of looking and listening, we said our good-byes and returned to our campsite. I looked at the RV hookups that had electricity and water and the nearby showers. It was hard to believe that some ten million years ago, woolly mammoths, mastodons, land turtles, prehistoric camels, and bone crushing dogs roamed this area. I also remembered reading that after Lake Fryer had been built disaster struck here in 1947 when floods washed out the dam and drained the lake. The area had returned to cattle grazing until 1954 when Ochiltree County obtained the land from the federal government and rebuilt the dam with local funds. Eddie interrupted my thoughts.

"Dinner's served, boys," he said.

Eddie had outdone himself in replenishing our calories. We had grilled pork chops topped with a sauce made from cranberries and raisins, hash browned potatoes, and a lettuce and tomato salad. After eating, I asked Eddie, a retired athletic trainer and trainer at the 1972 Olympics, to check my back, which had now developed a constant ache. He taped a hot pad that Norm had brought over the aching spot and showed me some new exercises to do.

As I felt the heat from the pad seep into my back, I thought about how glad we had Eddie on this trip. His knowledge of aches and ills brought on by walking had been learned during his many years as an athletic trainer. He had once told me that he had developed a love of the profession when he was a youngster and was not big enough to make the football team. He had become its manager. "I realized then that that was what I wanted to eventually become," he said. He had done well, serving as athletic trainer at Southern Methodist University under then coach Hayden Fry. The team had gone to the Cotton Bowl in 1966 and the Bluebonnet Bowl in 1968. He had also been chosen as an athletic trainer for the 1968 Olympics in Mexico City. As for the 1972 Olympics in Munich when the Black September terrorists kidnapped and killed six Israeli team members, Eddie said he remembered being about 200 yards away from where the shooting took place. "I could hear the shots and it sent fingers of fear running through me," he said.

Before we retired to our beds, Eddie said, "If your back is not much better in the morning, you better go see a doctor."

We went to bed about nine P.M. I listened to my radio and some station that was playing golden oldies. I went to sleep as the words from the song, "Till I waltz again with you, let no other hold your charms. I will keep my promise true, for you are my guiding light." I love to dance but after feeling the pain in my back, I didn't think I would be doing any dancing that night.

I woke up at one-thirty A.M. and checked my blood sugar. It was fine. I walked outside and looked up at the sky. A tiny film of clouds gently dulled the brilliant lights from the stars. I thought of the Indians who had once lived at this site and wondered what they thought when they looked at the sky and saw this burst of wonder. I went back to my sleeping bag and instantly fell asleep. I did not dream.

Chapter Five

So many days ended
With the moon shining bright
Our campfire flashing
Orange flames into the night.
Walk across Texas
With its beautiful sights
Walk across Texas
With its beautiful nights.

The owls sent me a wake-up call about seven A.M. My back felt like somebody had inserted a pinched wire down in the right hand corner. I decided not to join Eddie and Norm on the walk. Eddie gave me a series of exercises that he thought would help stretch the strained muscles in my back before they left.

I did the exercises and watched as two busloads of students unloaded across the lake. They screamed and ran toward the water. They stopped, picked up rocks and started throwing them, trying to skip the stones across the water. My stomach was also upset and I made three trips to the restroom facilities. As I walked back to the campsite, I thought, gosh, this is what they contended with in the old days.

I opened my notebook and read the previous day's recordings. I also read more history of the area. There was a short note I had made about not being able to make contact with John Erickson, author of the popular *Hank the Cowdog* children's books. Jane and I both loved his writing and had met him during a book festival at Austin. When I learned that he lived on a ranch in Ochiltree County, I thought what a great interview he would make and he might even invite us to camp out on his ranch.

I had written him an email and had tried to call him several times without success. He had sent me a long email response that he sends to all of his Hank fans, telling them how much he appreciated them taking the time to write him.

"I enjoy writing *Hank the Cowdog* books as much as you enjoy reading them," the email read.

Then he told about being a fifth generation Texan born in Midland (that's where I was raised) and living on an 8,500 acre ranch in Ochiltree County with his family, two dogs, an unknown number of cats, and about 300 cattle. He gets his ideas from watching his animals and said his cats are fun to watch and give him many good ideas for his Hank stories. But, he said nothing about a possible visit.

I had asked some of the people we had met the first day about Erickson. They said they knew him but that he was a very busy person. However, they said they would be glad to call him and try to arrange an interview for me. I told them thanks but I didn't think I had the time. Today, I wished I had taken them up on the offer. Aw well. So much for learning more about Hank the Cowdog.

I did some more stretching exercises and turned on my computer. I swore. The darn thing had gone on a blink, and a computer whiz I am not. So that meant I would not be able to write anything until Norm, the computer guru, returned. My back had a constant twinge in the right-hand corner. I fished out some of the stories about this area that Dr. T. Lindsay Baker had sent me and began reading them while fighting the blanket of black flies that abounded at our campsite.

I read one of Baker's stories about the vast herds of buffalo that had ranged over this area. The herds had once numbered in the tens of thousands. Then came the buffalo hunters with their big and powerful rifles and the demand for buffalo skins that were processed into leather for markets back east and in Europe. They did eat some of the choice parts of the buffalo, like the tongue and liver, but for the most part after removing the skin, they just left them lying in great piles. A draftsman for the U.S. Corps of Army Engineers had been sickened by the site and had written in a diary, "A mile from our camp we passed over a great many places where the buffalo hunters had made a stand and killed the animals up to twenty-five in a small place. The stench of the carcasses was awful."

I had listened to the coyotes singing their awful symphony at night. I thought of that this morning and remembered still another Baker story about Jack Abernathy who became known for his rather unusual way of capturing wolves that roam the region. Abernathy, a Bosque County native, did not use a trap for the sometimes wild and vicious animals. Instead, he rammed one of his hands down the animal's throat and grabbed hold of the lower jaw to prevent the wolf from chewing on the hand. He did not kill the animals and often provided them to zoos or to motion picture studios to be used in films. He became so well known that a hunt featuring Abernathy and his unusual technique was organized for viewing during a visit to the area by President Theodore Roosevelt.

Abernathy impressed the president so much that Roosevelt wrote about his wolf-catching abilities in his book, *Outdoor Pastimes of an American Hunter.* He told how Abernathy, riding a horse, kept the wolf heading in circles, slowing the animal down. Then just as the wolf crossed a creek, a dog used by Abernathy rushed the animal and penned it. The wolf bit the dog which let go and jumped back several feet. When this happened, Abernathy leaped from his horse and landed on top of the wolf. Then said the president, "While holding the reins from his horse in one hand, he thrust the other with a rapidity and precision even greater than the wolf's snap, into the wolf's mouth, jamming his hand down crosswise between the jaws, seizing the lower jaw and bending it down so the wolf could not bite him." The wolf had been successfully captured.

I looked up at the sky and saw some crows dive bombing for insects. I wondered if there were any characters like Jack Abernathy still roaming these parts. I would certainly like to meet them.

I kept reading until lunchtime. I made a sandwich and had a hard time eating it because of the flies. About an hour later Norm and Eddie drove up and told about their walk.

"I saw a red tail hawk. Gosh, they are so beautiful," said Norm. "It stayed on the electric pole until I got fairly close to it and then it went screeching off. I also walked across the Roberts' county line and the Canadian River."

Eddie told about seeing a herd of cattle.

"They acted like I should feed them some breakfast," he said. "I also saw a live two-foot rattler. He wasn't going to move until I used my walking cane to pitch him into the grass. I think he got a little mad at me."

Norm said two people had turned around and come back to make sure he didn't need any help. And, Al Lamm asked if he were Jon McConal.

"He was from Granbury and had read a story about our walk and is up in this country doing some work. He wanted to meet you," said Norm.

Eddie began cooking dinner. As he worked, he asked about my back. I told him I had done the exercises he had shown me before leaving that morning. I had also done some that a doctor had given to me about two months ago.

"I think I should go to a doctor in Perryton and have him check me out," I said. "I certainly do not want to call a halt to this. But, I have been thinking that we may have to make some adjustments. Maybe we could get Norm to become a member of the walking team and instead of us walking fifteen miles each, maybe we could each walk five miles and make some kind of arrangements where we could drive the car ahead and one of us walk to the car and then drive and pick up the others."

Norm walked over and listened.

"I certainly would be willing to do that," he said. "But, what would we do with the car?"

I put my notebook on the table and asked for him and Eddie to look at a plan I had devised. I explained it this way.

"I would be the first one on the fifteen mile section," I said. "Eddie would drop me and then drive ten miles ahead and drop you. Then he would drive back five miles and leave the car. Then he would begin his five-mile walk. When I reached the car, it would be at the end of my five miles. I would drive the car and pick up Eddie and then pick up you. That way we would have walked fifteen miles and if we follow the routine all of the way through, we will have walked the 450 miles."

Eddie and Norm studied my drawing.

"Makes sense," said Eddie. "But, what are we going to do if the doctor tells you that you can't walk any?"

I laughed.

"If he says that, then I will just do what my good friend Doug Clarke says to do in rough times," I said.

"Which is?" asked Norm.

"Suck it up and go tough," I said.

We all laughed. Eddie finished our dinner of grilled chicken, pinto beans, and salad. We ate and watched the stars come out. We went to bed early. I lay there and listened to the night sounds. I thought about my plans and decided that there was no way I was not going to make this trip. Far off I could hear the owl, who seemed to be agreeing with me.

Chapter Six

We passed mile sixty
We're still on the go
People smile at us
Saying, "Look at them go."
Walk across Texas
With its wonderful sights.
Walk across Texas
With its beautiful nights.

Eddie had awakened me several times one night battling with the raccoons who seemed intent on finding something to eat at our camp. They had ripped into a plastic bag of groceries the first night. We thought we had anchored everything down properly after that but never underestimate the power of a raccoon driven by hunger. They had torn off the end of a Styrofoam ice chest and had somehow managed to stick their claws inside and find some fruit.

Just after I had drifted off to sleep I had been awakened by an explosion of profanity from Eddie. I heard what I took to be the sound of somebody hitting a punching bag and Eddie saying, "Take that. I told you to get out of here."

So I was not surprised as I wandered around the campground waiting for the coffee to boil to see raccoon tracks in the dust on the rear glass of our vehicle. I looked at them and they reminded me of some child who had gotten a pencil and had scrawled some tracks in the dust. Eddie saw me and came over. "They were looking for something to eat," he said. "I'm glad I didn't leave the car keys lying outside on the table."

He asked me how my back felt. I told him not very good.

"Feels like it has a hot wire down there in the right side," I said. "I think I should go to the doctor."

We ate breakfast, loaded up, and drove to Perryton. We stopped at Jerry Whitehead's Chiropractic Health Clinic. His son, Jarel Whitehead, examined me and said I was badly in need of an adjustment. I didn't argue and allowed him to do his thing. I had to bite my teeth to keep from hollering a couple of times. But, after he had done a series of manipulations, he said he was done and that I should be able to continue my walking but that I should cut back on my daily mileage. His advice matched our revised plans so we drove to where we had stopped yesterday and continued our walking at an abandoned filling station that Norm had reached yesterday.

We all prowled around the structure that had a railroad gasoline tanker car painted silver sitting on concrete blocks outside the main building.

Trees grew out of cracks in the floors and walls of the structure. The strong wind slapped the limbs against the sides, making a lonely sound. I looked at the gasoline pumps in front. One had gasoline marked for 99.9 cents per gallon, which indicated the business had been closed for some-time. Inside pieces of sheetrock and insulation hung down like torn sheets of bandages from a giant wound. Had this station been somebody's dream and for some reason they had had to close the business and go back to society and an hourly paid job that promised them so much per week but offered nothing to grab onto at night when their body was aching from the hours of work but they don't really care about the pain because it came from working on something they own?

"Boys, we had better hit the road," said Eddie. "We are forty-three miles north of Pampa."

I looked at his map and the dot where he pointed. I looked down the line marking the road and saw the intersection of Highway 180 cutting into Highway 70 and then heading east and eventually leading us to Granbury. I felt a bit of concern as I thought about how much farther we had to walk. When you looked at the route on a highway map like this, well, it was a con-siderable distance.

But, we kept on heading south on this day. Because of my back, Norm had decided to walk with me. We walked past mesas and one that looked like an upside down mushroom. We walked past herds of cattle and far off in a distance I saw four horses running with the wind.

Streaks of pain began in my back. Norm moved in front of me, provid-ing a draft from the wind as we walked up a rather long and steep hill. He pointed at some mountains, hazy in the background, and then at a ranch house sitting on the side of a canyon that snaked through the foot of the mountains. The house was painted white and looked pretty sitting in the pasture with cattle and hills in the background.

"That would make a great weekend place for you, Norm," I said.

We kept walking and looked at the great abundance of sage growing in the pastures. It seemed like the wind had gotten stronger and as it hit the trees growing in the area it sounded like hot water being poured through a sieve in the process of making spaghetti. I looked at my watch and realized I had been walking for about ninety minutes. My back felt like it.

Again, I thought about this trip and how long Eddie and I had trained for it, getting our daily mileage average up to about six. I thought of all of the letters we had written to people living in the areas through which we would be walking and of plotting our daily destinations on maps. And, then, kapow, in just seconds of lifting up a darn ice chest in the wrong way, I had suddenly been made into a disabled participant. So I told Norm my back was really hurting and we drove to Eddie.

"Jon thinks he has had enough today," said Norm. "He wants us to continue and he will drive and look at the country and then pick us up."

"He wants to be supervisor dawg and drive the car," said Eddie.

We all laughed but agreed. I left them at their designated sections and began driving through the country. I looked at Dugout Creek and then crossed the Canadian River that had a wide shallow channel with a tiny twist of clear water. I drove on and reached the highway leading to Miami, which is the seat of Roberts County. At the site of old Parnell I read a historical marker that told some of the town's colorful history. Created in August 1876, Parnell remained unorganized as that year it had only one settler. Then the Santa Fe railroad came to this area and population increased. More efforts to organize a county were invalidated because of fraudulent voting. But, the disqualified officers opened a courthouse anyway in a vacant store in Miami twenty miles southeast of here.

The battle for the county seat continued and involved some rather unusual acts that included one group hiring a gunman to impersonate a landowner and capture a safe with election records stored inside. The safe was then hauled to the legal county seat near this site and set on blocks. A two-story frame courthouse was built around the safe and the county seat was declared to be located on the spot that became Parnell.

The town had twelve residences, a school, and a saloon. Those attending court had to camp, as the local hotel was small. Then came another effort to name Miami the county seat in 1898. It was successful, and Parnell was abandoned.

I looked at the site where I stood. A valley with several ranches in the background ran for several miles. Tumbleweeds grew in the fences. Their rusting red color warned about the coming of winter. Large clumps of Spanish Dagger grass, or what I call bare grass, grew in abundance. A man wearing jeans roared by on a four-wheeled vehicle. He waved his hat at me.

Across the pasturelands, elevations reached 3,210 feet in some places. The soil was black and sandy loam with clay and had mesquite and live oak trees growing in the waving flats of tall grasses. This country, like all of the surrounding area, got a severe punch during the Great Depression when the dust bowl covered the countryside. But even during those hard times a dream about gold and silver being buried somewhere in these vast surroundings kept people going. That dream started when Francisco Vasquez de Coronado and Hernando de Alvarado marched across the country in 1540. They were led by a Pawnee captive named El Turco who told them about a town in the distance that had many people who owned huge pots full of gold and silver.

The Spaniards kept marching until they came to a city that had only grass huts and a population who made their living by farming. They shook their heads in ignorance when asked about the gold and silver. The Spaniards confronted El Turco who admitted he had made the story up to keep the conquistadors away from his people. They killed him but his story became the essence of many stories of a city called Quivira where great caches of treasure were buried.

When looking at the vastness of this land and hearing the wind in its various stages ranging from whispers to rages, one can see why such stories endure even today. During my days at the *Star-Telegram* I wrote several stories about people who claimed to have found some document or heard some story that would lead them to the great Quivira. One rancher, with whom I spent several days on his property in far West Texas, even wore out several old bulldozers digging for the treasures over a plat of nearly a hundred acres. He had not found any of the gold and silver when I had last talked with him. But, he was still digging.

I smiled at those memories as I started the car and headed back for Highway 70 to pick up Norm and Eddie. We drove back to our campground and discussed our progress.

"I think we are doing okay," said Eddie. "We may be running a little behind but I think we can shorten some of our rest days and we will be on schedule."

I turned on the radio and tried unsuccessfully to find some popular music. That's like trying to find a dime in acres of scrap metal in this West Texas area. I finally settled on a country and western station and listened to some woman singing about how her man had done her wrong and she had taken him back and then he had done her wrong again and she had taken him back again and then he had done her wrong again and she finally had said, "Okay, Big Boy, I'm taking you back one more time."

I looked at Eddie wearing his black suspenders and canvas shorts and western hat. I thought about what we were doing and again felt good about the whole adventure. I wondered how many sixty-nine-year-old-men were sitting around a campsite drinking vodka and listening to the radio and the sounds of night. I looked at Norm who had just come back from the showers, his white hair and beard glistening from the water. With his face reddened by the sun and wind after our first days of walking, he looked like Santa Claus or Ernest Hemingway.

I remembered a story Norm had told me about getting involved in skydiving. He had been stationed at SAC headquarters in Omaha and had mentioned to one of his friends that he had always wanted to make a parachute jump. "He quickly introduced me to a master sergeant who happened to be the president of a nearby skydiving club. We talked for an hour or two. I went through an orientation Friday after work and did ground school and my first jump on Saturday. I was hooked," he said.

He said his jump club made many demonstration jumps. Most of those were made without the parachutists getting a chance to look at the landing area before the jump. That resulted in one of Norm's most memorable jumps at Ames, Iowa, where he was supposed to land in a football stadium.

"As I approached the stadium and being maybe still 300 feet in the air, it became apparent that the stadium lights which I intended to fly between were connected by power lines. I barely managed to clear the wires, drop down quickly, and do a one foot standup in front of the crowd," he said. He smiled. "They never knew the closeness of that call but the pucker factor was extreme."

He talked about the risk involved in skydiving. "Let's start this by talking about a death wish so many people think that skydivers have. Jumpers don't have it," he said. "What jumpers do have is a love of thrills and an affinity for adrenaline." He finished by talking about the danger of skydiving. "Beyond any doubt, skydiving is inherently dangerous, but not nearly so much as people assume," he said. "I'd estimate that the odds of making a fatal jump, based purely on statistics, are 50,000 to one. I've lost friends in cars, never in skydiving accidents. Like plane crashes, they make great press," he said. "Safe jumps hardly ever do."

As I looked at our camping site, I realized that this was the first night there were any campers beside us at the lake. The smell of several campfires and the sight of a full moon hanging over the eastern sky made for a nice setting. My back still felt tender but better than it had before.

"I'm going to do a little packing tonight because we are going to have to move camp tomorrow," said Eddie.

As the hours faded on our fifth night, Norm talked about walking into new territory tomorrow. "Isn't it neat to find something like that old filling station and be able to mess around in its remains," he said. He sipped a drink of scotch. "Now, if we were just speeding down the highway, we would never have even noticed it."

I agreed. I watched as he and Eddie set up their cots and stretched their blankets and sleeping bags over them. The wind had died. They both said goodnight and crawled onto their cots, made a few more adjustments, snorted, and then silence settled over the area. I stayed up a few more minutes and watched the moon creep overhead, chasing away shadows from the trees and picnic table and creating others as the sides not illuminated by the moonlight grew long and black. I finally crawled into the Highway Hilton that really was not much more than three four-by-eight sheets of plywood hinged and bolted together. I pulled my sleeping bag to the center of the air mattress and climbed inside, listening to the creaks and moans of the bolts and screws as I tried to make myself comfortable.

I finally reached a comfortable position and lay there listening to the night. Norm and Eddie were snoring. Maybe they would keep the raccoons scared away tonight.

Chapter Seven

We saw West Texas toughness
In all kinds of places
We saw abandoned homes
And old rusting gas stations.
Walk across Texas
With its wonderful sights.
Walk across Texas
With its beautiful nights.

Last night's weather forecast brought a small change in our plans. The weather person had predicted temperatures in the upper thirties and heavy thundershowers. We knew that our camping rig was not equipped to handle such conditions so we decided to stay in our first motel in Pampa for the next few nights. As we made our last preparations to leave this camping site, Norm looked at some of the campers who had arrived the night before.

"Well, here's an interesting phenomenon," he said. "We have people coming to camp in $20,000 campers. And, right beside them is somebody else in a $30,000 camper. And the other interesting thing, they haven't been outside since they got here."

We had watched their arrivals and made humorous remarks as they set up their rigs and turned on the water and electricity that made the long, huge trailers blink with lights that looked like a small house. We had listened as they pulled down their windows and turned on their air conditioners, which panted regularly like distance runners throughout the night.

"That's really camping out," said Eddie. "I mean that is really experiencing the outdoors."

So began our sixth day. My back felt better but twinges of pain still shot through it so I decided to take another day off from walking a long distance. One of our last acts of packing came when Eddie took one of Norm's hot packs and duct-taped it to my back.

"Duct tape is the baling wire of the baby boomers," he said.

We hooked up the Highway Hilton and headed south for Pampa. We passed a huge flock of buzzards circling near some rock cliffs. I wondered if they had spotted breakfast and remembered days when I was a youngster and living on a ranch and would ride our pastures searching for missing cattle or calves. A flock of buzzards circling could be bad news and I always rode to the point where they were flying to check and see if that missing animal might be lying dead near the site.

I let Eddie out and then drove five miles down the road and let Norm out. I told him I would pick him up in about an hour and a half. I drove through Gray County, which is in the central part of the Panhandle, on the eastern edge of the High Plains. The ground was level and had sandy loam and black soils on which grew native grasses and farming crops like wheat, corn, grain sorghum, and hay. I looked at a winding creek cutting across the countryside and noticed cottonwood, hackberry, elm, and mesquite growing near the banks.

Pampa is the seat of Gray County and the largest town in the county. The local chamber called the city of some 20,000 the "Friendly City at the Top of Texas where the wheat grows and the oil flows." Oil was discovered in 1926 and as a result, Godfrey L. Cabot, head of Cabot Carbon in Boston, established the first of several carbon black plants in the area. The name Pampa was selected for the city because the place resembled the pampas of Argentina where an early settler had once visited.

I found a pullout on the highway and parked. I sat for a while and looked at the pasturelands that extended on and on. I thought about what the members of the Coronado Expedition had said about the area during their 1541 expedition when they were seeking the riches of Quivira. In his report to the King of Spain after his return to Mexico, Coronado said, "I reached some plains with no more landmarks and looked as if we had been swallowed up in a sea . . . there was not a stone, nor a bit of rising ground, nor a tree, nor a shrub, nor anything to go by."

Pedro de Castaneda, another member of the expedition, said he had never seen anything like the incredible flatness of the terrain and that the country reminded him of a bowl. "When a man sits down, the horizon surrounds him all around at a distance of a musket shot," he wrote.

The Coronado expedition was not small. It had more than a thousand men and thousands of animals that were moved along with the group. But, Castaneda said that neither the men nor the animals brought change to the ground over which they walked.

"Who could believe that 1,000 horses and 500 of our cows and more than 5,000 rams and ewes and more than 1,500 friendly Indians and servants in traveling over those plains, would leave no more trace where they had passed as if nothing had been there—nothing," he wrote.

As a matter of fact, the group made such little impact on the ground that efforts had to be made to fashion piles of buffalo bones and dung so that the rear guard would know where to march. "The grass never failed to become erect after it had been trodden down," said Castaneda, "And, although it was short, it was as fresh and straight as before."

I looked at the rolling grasslands and thought about the 1852 Red River Expedition made by Captain Randolph Barnes Marcy and George Brinton McClellan. That expedition of some fifty-five explorers proved several things. One was that the Red River's headwaters came from several of the wet-dry creeks in the Pampa area and that the 1,222 mile long stream ran east and south before emptying into the Mississippi River.

But the main thing the expedition proved was that this rugged country could be settled and pioneers could indeed wrestle a living from the area. The premise that civilization depended on land, water, and timber was proven even though the efforts at finding those required determination and strength that would be pushed to the limits.

I looked at my watch and saw it was time to pick up Eddie and Norm. After they climbed into the car, I told them I wanted to check out a sign that I had passed on the highway. We drove back and read the sign that said, "Cottonwood Springs Guest Ranch. Cabins, weddings, parties."

"We might get us a camping site here," I said as I headed down the gravel road leading from the highway. The road led down a hillside and in the distance we could see a winding creek with several cottonwood trees growing along its banks. We kept driving and after about a mile we reached a large log house with a wrap-around front porch. An old freight wagon sat in the front yard along with a pickup and a surburban. I walked up the stairs and knocked several times. No answer. I knocked again and looked at a flock of wild turkeys running across the backyard. The wind swept through the tall native grasses growing in abundance a short distance from the house. I looked inside a window and could not see anyone. So I said what the heck and walked back to the car.

"Let's go," I said.

"It would have been a nice place to settle for a night or two," said Eddie.

Aw, what the hell. We drove on into Pampa and rented some rooms at the Best Western. The afternoon still had plenty of sun before darkness so we explored the town. We quickly found an interesting place called Radcliff's Rocks and Relics sitting on Highway 70 on the south side of town. You can't miss it. A green dinosaur with yellow eyes and a purple Barney sit in the front along with hubcaps, old bottles, and pieces of aging farm equipment.

"It's a disaster," said the owner, Jim Radcliff, sixty-six. He's slender and wears jeans and a baseball cap. His face is creased with two scars. He invited us to look as much as we wanted and offered explanations about the concrete animals in the front of his place.

"My daughter, her name is Renda Vandenberg, made them dinosaurs. She gave me one as a Father's Day present," he said. He laughed. "Now wasn't that a unique gift?" He didn't wait for an answer. He continued, "There is about 1,500 pounds of mortar mix in them. And she is down on the creek making another one today. But these that are here, well she just

Jon Mcconal, left, talks with Jim Radcliff of Pampa, at Radcliff's Rocks and Relic shop in Pampa. The green dinosaur weighs 3,000 pounds and was built by his daughter, Renda Vandenburg. Photos by Eddie Lane and Norm Snyder.

made them out of stuff she could find. Like his eyes, they are old light bulbs that we found. And the teeth came from an old rake. She made them claws from a pitchfork. Now this one here beside him, he started out as a sawhorse. His teeth are real cow's teeth and real cow's horns. Ha. Ha. We just went out and chopped them off with a hack saw."

He laughed again and continued. "That body came from a barbecue pit and his legs are tomato cages. She just bent them around and wired it all together. Took us two days to put that concrete in there and every two years, she comes back home and paints them for me."

He said he calls one of the dinosaurs Cliff and the other one Rad.

"Old Rad, he's got marble eyes," he said. He stared at the front space of the business that is getting kind of crowded with stuff. "Yeah, I need some more space so the next thing I get may be just a big old spider."

I pointed at a huge rock and asked where it came from.

"That's not just a rock. It's a piece of flint," he said. "As a matter-of-fact, it's the biggest piece of flint in Pampa. Weighs 900 pounds. Nobody's got one any bigger."

He said before he retired seven years ago and opened this place, he worked as a gasoline plant operator. He was born in Borger, which is twenty-six miles away.

"I've been able to buy everything I wanted without going anywhere," he said. "Like I got the biggest variety of cactus in town. I've got thirty-nine

A close-up of Renda Vandenberg's Rad and Cliff, at Radcliff's Rocks and Relics shop in Pampa. Photos by Eddie Lane and Norm Snyder.

different kinds of cactus. I give them away. You know like Johnny Appleseed gave away apples. Well, I give cactus away."

So does he like his work? He eyed me like that was a stupid question.

"Listen, this sure beats being a door greeter at Wal-Mart," he said. "I live on Social Security. But, wait until I get a bunch of good arrowheads and then business will really go up. Yeah, it will."

He introduced us to his wife, Yvonne, and their dog, a poodle named Napoleon. Yvonne confided, "We've got a little bit of everything. But, what I like is all of our blue glass."

"Hey, you know something about us. We are at the crossroads of the world. In other words, we are the center of the universe, if you know what I mean," he said.

Since we stood in piles of rocks, stacks of plastic toys, and racks of marbles, I couldn't disagree. I petted Napoleon. He blinked his eyes at bridle bits, spurs, and pieces of barbed wire.

We told them about our walk. They seemed impressed. Yvonne asked, "Do you walk all night?"

"No, lady, there is no way that we walk at night," said Norm.

Then Jim started talking about his daughter again.

"She is studying to be a paramedic up in Olympia, Washington. I really didn't want them dinosaurs, but she got bored and started making them as a surprise for me," he said. He smiled. "And, I kinda like them now. They are eye catchers."

"That is a slight understatement," said Norm.

"Say, let me give you some advice," said Jim. "If y'all want to see something that is kinda off your trail you are walking but sure is worth a visit, go by Groom and look at the cross there. That thing stretches several hundred feet up into the air. Made out of steel and it is really worth going to see."

He gave us directions to Groom.

"It's about thirty miles from here. You get close to Groom and you can't miss the cross. You can see it for forty miles away from some places. I think it was built by a football player, but I am not sure," he said. "But, it's worth making an effort to go see it."

We thanked them and started to leave. Yvonne gave us one last word of advice.

"You boys don't get run over," she said.

We drove back to the motel and went to our rooms. I took a shower and found myself feeling the sheets and the air coming out of the air conditioner. I laughed at my efforts. I had only been away from indoor delights for five days and I was acting like I had not had them for months.

We retired to our rooms early. A cold north wind hammered the ground and sheets of rain pounded the windows. I looked at the television but did not turn it on. Instead, I read some from a paperback novel that I had bought at a used bookstore. I fell asleep about ten P.M. I missed hearing the owls sing.

Chapter Eight

We walked beside wheat fields
And past pastures full of grass
We walked past cotton fields
And past wells pumping gas.
Walk across Texas
With its wonderful sights.
Walk across Texas
With its beautiful nights.

The giant cross at Groom can be seen from miles away as we learned on our side trip for a view of this spectacle.

"There it is," said Eddie. He pointed to the large cross looming out of the haze several miles in front of us. We kept driving until we reached Groom and the parking lot near the cross. Many vans, pickups, automobiles, semi-truck rigs, and motorcycles had stopped for a view. I climbed from the car and literally had to lean backwards to see the top of the steel structure, which stretched upwards some nine stories or 190 feet.

A large paved circle reached out from the cross. Along its outward edges were the seven Stations of the Cross sculptured in bronze with plaques explaining each one. I stopped at another monument dedicated to the loving "memory of the innocent victims of abortion." I walked around the circle and then went inside the gift shop where people have written messages on a legal pad. One asked for prayers for "my son for his diabetes."

I talked to Belinda Scott, a volunteer who has worked at the gift shop for five years. She told about Steve Thomas, president of Caprock Engineering in Pampa, who designed the cross and used his own money to build it on ten acres of donated land. It was completed in July 1995 and it was Thomas's way of giving back to the Lord, she said.

While she tended to some customers, I read more messages. One asked for "help for Machina. He is in Boston for a cancer and heart surgery. Please pray for him. His daughter and best friend."

I looked at plates for sale with scriptural messages written on them. I also looked at a book that included 101 ways to love your grandkids and at scripture key rings. Then I talked to Belinda's father, Freddy Martinez, who was filled with enthusiasm about being able to serve as a volunteer at the cross. He told about working here when a church brought some hot air balloons for a celebration.

"Oh, god, it was so pretty," he said. "They do things like that every holiday and oh, my god, it's so impressive and so pretty and they come over here and bring their choirs from their churches and they sing and it is just beautiful."

Jon McConal and his walking partners made a side trip to Groom to look at the 190-foot tall cross that contains seventy-five tons of steel. Steve Thomas of Pampa erected the cross in 1995. Photos by Eddie Lane and Norm Snyder.

He's a short man with black hair tinged with gray. He said he knows what it is to believe in God and do hard work and be rewarded from prayer.

"Oh yeah. When I was a kid I used to pick cotton. I was six when I started. Oh yes, I also chopped cotton. You'd wear your knees off. We'd pick cotton until our fingers started freezing and then we'd keep on picking until we got 500 pounds in our sacks and then maybe we would take a break," he said. "But, I kept working and praying and I got a job out of the cotton patch and then I did pretty good and now I can volunteer at the cross and hear all of that beautiful music during holidays."

I looked some more and then joined Eddie and Norm outside. They both leaned back and looked at the top of the cross. "It is one tall creation," said Norm.

We drove to nearby Groom with its wide streets and grain elevators and a Route 66 Steak House. We ate lunch and then drove across the Canadian River and stopped at a historical marker that told about the Eldridge Post Office having been there once. Its establishment saved ranchers having to ride twenty miles to Clarendon or thirty miles to Mobeetie to mail letters. Nearby stood a massive live oak tree with huge limbs and a giant girth. I wondered if it had ever been a hanging tree. I later asked a native of the area who said he did not know but he would not have been surprised because they did once hang people around here.

We stopped after driving across North McLelland Creek. I rolled down the window and the sound of flies immediately came from the outside. We looked and could not see a feedlot, but I did roll up the window.

"Sounds like our campground back at Perryton," said Eddie.

We drove to Lefors, a population 559, which had once been the seat of Gray County. We passed several vacant buildings and a house with a fence made out of steel wagon wheels. A sign proclaimed that this was the home of the Pirates, which I assumed was the mascot of the local high school team. The courthouse had once been a two-story frame structure that was built for less that $2,500. The town profited in those days from the oil boom but Pampa became the county seat in one of those bitterly fought elections in 1928. But, Lefors is still popular for the annual Lost in Lefors Poker Run, a motorcycle race in which a Harley Davidson motorcycle is given away after a day of activities held every August.

Black clouds gathered in the north as we headed back to Pampa. We crossed Thut Creek and then drove across miles of pastureland before arriving in Pampa. We stopped at the Freedom Museum USA that had a helicopter, an artillery piece, a half-track, and a B-25 in a fenced in area. It was closed.

I had wanted to visit and read about the Pampa Army Air Field, a World War II military base built in 1942 about eleven miles east of Pampa.

It became known as the Eagles' Nest of the High Plains and offered advanced twin-engine training in AT-17s. Also stationed at the field were B-25s, sixteen of which took part in the bombing of Tokyo. During its three years, the base graduated 6,292 cadets, trained 3,500 aircraft mechanics and had one of the best safety records in the U.S. Training Command throughout the war. It was abandoned after its closing in 1943.

We reached our motel as thunder sounded in the north. As we unloaded, rain began again. We ran to our rooms as the rain intensified. I pulled my curtains and looked out in the light that was fading quickly. I thought of our experiences that day.

It had begun with a weather report that had not sounded good for three old codgers walking along Texas highways on this day. More rain and weather in the upper fifties were forecast for two days. We decided to stay at the motel another night but go ahead and try to walk.

Eddie drove us to our stations and we began walking. I could hear the sounds of an airplane and a train in the background as I walked down Highway 70. I had dressed in several layers so I was not uncomfortable. I smelled the powerful odors of grass reinvigorated by last night's rain and of hay waiting to be mowed and bailed. I walked past a windmill that had no blades. A sign with fading paint hung precariously from near the tower's top. It read, "Cole Green Antiques and Collectibles."

I kept walking and reached a huge gate made from pipe. A sign on the gate read, "House for sale. $5,000 firm." I looked at the framed structure painted a rusting brown color. It had a white picket fence on the front porch. The front screen door had several busted places and hung at an angle. A row of what looked like brass hearts or twisted metal ribbons ran along the top of the roof and down the edge of the house. I figured that they must have been some kind of protection from lightning and remembered stories I had heard about lightning rod salesmen traveling the countryside selling their latest models.

I walked another mile and came upon a mother cow outside of the fence. Her calf on the other side bawled as it ran up and down the fence looking for a way to its mother. The mother eyed me suspiciously. I stayed several feet away and kept my arms at my sides. Finally, she snorted and began to follow the calf until she came to a place where the fence wires sagged down so much they created a kind of hole. She stuck her head through the wire and then, almost like she knew what she was doing, she climbed through the wires. The calf immediately ran to her udder and began nursing.

A couple hundred yards from this scene stood a historical marker that told about Captain Randol B. Marce and George McClellan riding through this area in the 1840s trying to locate the headwaters of the Red River. A field of cotton that had been harvested lay beyond the marker. A wind caught tiny pieces of the cotton and sent them on a crazy, almost dance-like twirl across the land.

I reached the car, had a long drink of water and then drove to pick up Norm. He got in and said that Al Lamm of Granbury had again stopped to talk to him.

"He still wanted to meet you," said Norm. "He said he was up in this country driving a combine for a harvesting company. He gave me his card to give to you."

We picked up Eddie. We had completed our fifteen miles for the day and decided that we would make a side trip to Groom and visit the cross that Jim Radcliff had told us about. As we drove west, last night's rain stood in evidence by the several playa lakes in the fields and pastureland.

I had first become aware of these lakes that abound after heavy rainfall in this part of Texas when I was a youngster living in the Midland area. We had leased some ranchland between Midland and San Angelo. One day after a rain that had measured three inches we drove to the property to check on our cattle. Shortly after we entered the ranch, I saw this huge lake stretching out in front of us. I could not believe it because I knew it had not been there the previous week when we had been here to vaccinate some calves.

"That's what is called a playa lake, Bunky," my dad had told me. "They only show up after a good, hard rain like we had last night and yesterday. They'll last maybe a month or two and then dry up again."

The landowner had brought a boat with a large outboard motor to speed around the lake. That was the first outboard motor I had ever seen. Daddy had parked the pickup and we watched as the man roared across the water, sending up showers of water. He saw us and motored to the shoreline where we had parked.

"Damn, Mack, ain't this something," he said. He lifted the outboard motor to a slant. He hit the accelerator and it roared like an angry bull. I put my hands to my ears to stop the noise. "I love this boat. But, I don't ever get it out except when it rains and one of these lakes happens. But, it is a helluva lot of fun."

I had read about the playas while doing research for this book. Early inhabitants said they were caused when herds of buffalo stopped and wallowed around in an area. But, research has shown that the playas originated from the strong winds that battered the landscape, literally scooping out the bowl-shaped basins.

The word playa came from the early Spanish explorers and means beach. The lakes, which number about 19,000 in the Texas High Plains, can reach sizes of more than 200 acres. But, the average size is about seventeen acres. Most basins remain dry until runoffs from a rainstorm. Without frequent rain, they soon dry up and remain that way until another rain soaks the area.

Spearheads traced back to the Folsom or a Folsom-like culture have been dug from a bed of elephant bones discovered in an ancient playa in Roberts County. Coronado and his troops became the first persons to mention the playas in their sixteenth-century walk across the territory. He said his men often were forced to drink from what they called the "buffalo wallows." And, although they were not reliable sources for drinking water because they dried out fairly quickly, they caused problems for early explorers when they had to walk around them when they did contain water.

Playa basins became important sources of hay near the turn of the century because the heavy clay soils held onto moisture even in dry years. Cattlemen bought hundreds of bales of hay that came from the playas and preferred it because they thought the hay was superior. In years of normal rainfall, the playas are important wintering grounds for waterfowl in the Central Flyway and attract more than a million mallards and other birds including large numbers of ring-necked pheasants that come to the playas to eat.

I listened to the rain hitting the windows in my room, sounding like somebody had thrown handfuls of metal pellets against them. I was glad we were not camping out that night.

Chapter Nine

We saw many unusual things
As we walked from the west
Like in Miami, Texas
They have a cow-calling contest.
Walk across Texas
With its wonderful sights.
Walk across Texas
With its beautiful nights.

With the wind hitting twenty miles an hour and the temperature hovering near forty degrees, we did not have a hard time deciding to take the day off and make a side trip to Miami, home of the National Cow Calling Contest since 1949. I had called Barbara Alexander who handles the planning for the annual event and she sounded excited that we would visit the city of about 600 people.

We drove through the rolling plains covered with tall native grasses and mesquite and live oak trees. Numerous little creeks drained into the Canadian River and its tributaries. Plains Apaches once roamed this area until they were pushed out by the Comanches, who hunted the immense herds of buffalo until Colonel Ranald S. Mackenzie and his federal troops defeated the Indians in the Red River War of 1874–1875.

Miami, the seat of Roberts County, supposedly derives its name from an Indian word meaning sweetheart. The city uses the name in its advertisements, calling itself the sweetheart of the plains.

We stopped in the downtown area at the old Miami Railroad Depot, erected in 1888. The site, which once had a tent hotel, has several old railroad luggage carts sitting outside, looking like they could still be piled with huge stacks of luggage and rolled to waiting trains. After a few minutes, we retreated to the car and started the heater.

"I think the temperature must have dropped to the thirties," said Norm as he blew onto his hands for warmth.

We waited until Barbara Alexander arrived and she invited us into the senior citizens' center to talk about the cow calling contest and Miami.

"We're just a little town but we have a lot of fun during the contest, which is held every June," she said.

William Jackson, who owns a garage in the downtown area, agreed.

"The contest is just a big old hollering match," he said. "It's a reunion time for family members who have moved off to come back and see their families and friends. A couple of local ranchers usually win it. They're not big men but they are loud and can really belt out a cattle call."

Jackson helps with the weekend of entertainment by dressing up like a woman with several of his buddies and doing skits on Friday night.

"Last year we did a take off on 'Hee-Haw.' Folks seemed to get a kick out of us," he said. "But, enter the cow calling contest . . . no sir, I don't do that. I may get up on the stage all dressed up like a woman and act silly but I am not going to get up in front of a bunch of people and start calling cows."

Alexander laughed at her friend. He may not have the courage to get up and call cattle in front of people but there are lots of other folks who like to enter the contest.

"We had a man come in from Utah last year to call," she said. "We have events for men, women, and children. The first place winners get $50. But, it's mainly for fun."

Jackson said the judges are stationed two blocks away. The contestants are told to face the direction in which the judges are sitting and then start calling.

"They cup their hands over their mouths and just belt it out until they turn red in the face," he said.

As we talked, Leslie D. Espinosa, publisher and editor of the local newspaper, the *Miami Chief,* walked inside and introduced herself. She said she has owned the paper, which is more than a hundred years old, for about a month. Before that she worked as an assistant to the county judge and county attorney.

"And, one of my hobbies is taking pictures," she said. "So when the woman who owned the *Chief* decided she wanted to sell it, she told me that there was nobody else better suited to buy it. So I bought it and I like putting it out."

We said our good-byes and drove toward Clarendon, our next stop. We passed through Alanreed, a tiny community with several vacant buildings including an old Phillip's 66 Service Station. We looked at the old gasoline pumps and noted that the station sat only a short distance away from some remainders of old Route 66.

We arrived at Clarendon and stopped at Sam Hill's Barbecue, with a sign advertising "Larruping Good Steaks." As we ate, we talked with some cowboys sitting at the next table. Eddie told them about our walk and asked how far it was to Turkey.

"You gonna walk all the way to Turkey," one of them said. He shook his head. "That's forty miles. That's a long walk. But let me tell you something. You want to watch out for them hawgs."

"Hawgs?" asked Eddie.

"Yeah, hawgs. Like in wild hawgs. They've become really bad around here, particularly at night," he said.

"We don't walk at night," said Norm.

"Well, you still want to be careful of the hawgs. Particularly if you see one of them old sows that has pigs. You see that and you git yourself away from her. She'll do anything to protect her pigs," he said.

We thanked him and paid our bill. Light rain peppered the windshield and the temperature still rested near forty. We decided to stay in a motel again. After we had checked in, I listened to the rain that had become heavier. I looked outside. A heavy lid of darkness dropped just beyond the motel lights. I thought about how far we had come and remembered looking down the highway south and realizing how vast and rugged this country was. But, the view did not depress me. I knew we would complete our walk.

Chapter Ten

Sometimes we got homesick
Then we'd look into the skies
And, suddenly we knew
We were three lucky guys.
Walk across Texas
With its wonderful sights.
Walk across Texas
With its beautiful nights.

The almost instant response this country makes to a rain could be seen as we began our eighth day of walking. Where brown had been the predominant color of the countryside only yesterday, today the pastures and grain fields flashed vividly like a traffic light hung on the green cycle. The trees appeared darker and at first I attributed this to the rain but decided after walking a mile that it came because of lack of sunshine.

I looked down the highway digging into the land in front of me. It stretched on and on like a dull piece of duct tape. I could not help but become a bit depressed as I looked at the length of the road over which we must walk until we reached Highway 180 and turned east. I had forgotten how many miles Eddie said we had walked as we ate breakfast that morning. But, I knew it was a long way from being halfway and certainly a long way from our final goal of 450.

Officially our walk reached Donley County yesterday. But, we still had not walked to Clarendon, where we had stayed last night. We were about twenty miles from its city limits. We had considered staying at Greenbelt Lake. But, after hearing another weather forecast of rain and temperatures in the thirties and looking at the limited camping facilities at the lake, we had decided to stay in a motel. We drove back to our starting point and began walking the twenty miles to Clarendon.

As I walked across the land of sandy clay and deep and sandy loam, I thought about some of the characters who had once called this country home. One of those was Asa Elmer Reid Jr., who became known as Ace Reid, a cowboy cartoonist and a delightful character. As a youngster, he had helped his father work cattle on the family ranch at Lelia Lake. He was a good cowboy, but early on he said he would rather spend his time drawing horses than riding them. In his last two years in high school, he built an art studio out of what had once been an old chicken house.

He quit school in 1943 and joined the navy. He served in the Pacific and visited Nagasaki a month after the atomic bomb had been dropped there. He came back to the Panhandle after the war and eventually became a cowboy artist and cartoonist. That was after he had been diagnosed with leukemia as a result of his visit to Nagasaki. That diagnosis was made in 1961 and Reid was given only five years to live. The diagnosis didn't slow him down. He and his wife moved to Kerrville where they bought a ranch and called it the Draggin' S Ranch. That was about the time I met him when he visited the *Star-Telegram* where the late George Dolan, a longtime *Star-Telegram* columnist, became his friend. Reid's storytelling made him almost as famous as his cartoons that earned him the label of being the "Texas Pen and Ink Will Rogers." He died November 10, 1991.

My thoughts were interrupted when a pick-up stopped and the driver rolled down his window. He hollered, "Want a ride?"

"Naw," I said. "I'm on a walk."

"A walk?" asked the driver.

"Yeah," I said. "A walk across Texas."

"How far across Texas?" he asked.

"Oh, about 450 miles," I said.

"Gawd, that's a whole bunch," he said. He smiled and shook his head. "Well, I don't guess you need a ride. So I'll see you on down the road."

I kept walking and passed the Jericho Cemetery that had its first documented burial in 1895. There were many tombstones of victims of smallpox and influenza epidemics. A marker said that the town of Jericho had been a station on the Chicago, Rock Island, and Gulf rail line.

We reached our fifteen-mile destination about ten miles north of Clarendon. Heavy clouds made a dark gray blanket to the south of us. The wind had increased. I looked at the countryside and saw in it a beauty that one would not catch while driving down the highway. Standing there and watching the formation of the clouds and the striking colors from the ranch houses and isolated pieces of farm equipment sitting in the fields made me think of a fine oil painting. If we had been just driving through, it might have looked like a photograph but not a painting.

We decided to visit nearby Hedley. That came from a suggestion made by Martha and Douglas Lowe, longtime Clarendon residents and friends of Marsha and Phil Delucchi in Granbury. The Lowes are a delightful, friendly couple and knew loads of history about the area and Clarendon, the county seat founded by Lewis Henry Carhart, a young Methodist minister.

Carhart and his brother-in-law, W.A. Allen, established Clarendon in 1878 as a Christian colony in the Texas Panhandle that discouraged liquor consumption and other impure activities. Methodist ministers soon numbered more than half a dozen and the settlement became known by cowboys passing through as the "Saint's Roost" because of the lack of sinful activities. The town became a sobriety settlement and its reputation as a conservative enclave with educational facilities earned it the label of "the Athens of the Panhandle." And, the last legal hanging in the Panhandle took place in Clarendon on June 3, 1910. I asked the Lowes how they liked living in such a conservative city.

"Oh, we love it," she said. "We've got twelve or fifteen churches here and I think that is wonderful. I was gone from here for thirty-seven years, but it was always home to me. Living here, well you know everybody and everybody knows you. Let me give you an example. My air conditioner broke about five P.M. on a Saturday. I called the air conditioning man and he was here in fifteen minutes. And, if you leave the light on in your garage, the sheriff will call and ask if you are all right and did you know that the light was on in your garage. And, no we don't have liquor around here. We may have a few drunks but they have to import the liquor in."

She then gave me a list of things we should see while staying here, including Clarendon Junior College, the oldest continuous operating junior college in Texas, and the Moffitt Hardware and Feed Store in Hedley. So that is why we headed to Hedley. We passed a very large feedlot operation which Eddie called the largest he had ever seen. I agreed. The cattle standing at the feed troughs numbered more than 1,000.

We drove into Hedley and saw a sign advertising the Lioness Club and Big Mom's Café. We parked in front of Moffitt's, a white concrete-block building. We walked inside and met Bill Carson, owner. Eddie told him about our walk and that we could not pass up a hardware store like his with its old hardwood floors and a variety of items for sale.

"It's been here since 1917 when Mister Hobert Moffitt opened it. I've owned it the past fifteen years," Carson said. "See those steel ceiling tiles, well, a man came in from Houston and said that tile was worth more than the whole building."

He and his wife Juanell owned a lumberyard in Borger before moving here. But, because he had trouble finding help, he sold that business and decided to retire.

"Juanell was born here so we moved back," he said. "We live on the place where she was born. Anyway, this place came up for sale, and my daughter said retirement is not in my vocabulary, so we bought it."

He pointed at antique machinery pieces hanging on a wall. "My daughter sees something so she buys it and brings it in here and hangs it on the wall," he said. "I do the same. Take those old cotton gin scales. They will weigh a 500-pound bale of cotton. I bought those."

The wall also has old saws, shovels with one-piece wooden handles, an old tank made out of a kerosene cook stove, harnesses, and a bucket once used to pull water from a well. And there is an aging corn planter that has a container for seed corn. The seed was placed in that and then the contraption was pushed down the row and every time the farmer pulled the handle one of the seeds fell from the container and down into the ground.

I moved along the aisles and looked at car batteries, Western Electric fence insulators, and a roll of Polaroid film with an expiration date of December 1999. The film's price tag was $4.99. I stopped and talked to Mrs. Carson and Betty Morgan.

"I went to school outside of town at a place called Quail. Our girl's basketball team was called the Bob Whites," said Mrs. Carson. "Enjoy it? Oh, sometimes. But, sometimes I'd rather be in Amarillo or some place that has some nice restaurants."

Mrs. Morgan smiled and said she had lived there since 1945 and does not know what the local citizenry would do without the hardware store. She said she worked for the original owner. She pointed to a room in an upstairs portion of the building.

"I used to work for Hobert. He kept the Christmas toys up there. I remember how much the youngsters used to love to come here for Christmas shopping and get to go up those stairs and look at the toys," she said. "Hobert also liked to watch trains when they came in. He loved the old steam engines. They told a story about him that said he got so absorbed watching the steam engines one day that the train ran into him. When they did away with the steam engines, he really got depressed."

Mrs. Carson pointed to a picture of an old freight train pulling a red caboose across the countryside with smoke pouring from the steam engine. "That was in Hobert's house. We got possession of it and hung it on the wall because that was a fitting place for it," she said.

I walked to the back and looked at creaking, antique wooden cabinets with wooden drawer handles filled with latches, bolts, and nuts. Steel rectangular shaped washtubs were stacked on top of the cabinets along with copper tubing, fan belts, rakes, and mixings for wallpaper seam repair. I stopped at a huge old steel wood-burning stove and could imagine the heat it produced during the winter months.

"They generally have some peanuts sitting on top of that roasting," she said. "People come in and sit and eat roasted peanuts and talk."

After an hour of looking, we all shook hands and promised to return when we were back in this country and maybe sit and eat some of the peanuts. The Carsons said we would be welcome.

We drove back to Clarendon. We stopped at the courthouse and Eddie took a photograph of the stately looking old building with a roof painted red and trim painted yellow. The community had placed massive granite markers for the veterans of the Korean War, World Wars I and II, and Vietnam near the courthouse.

We listened to the weather report that more rain and colder temperatures were coming. Jane and Barbara were also coming the next day. So we decided to stay in the motel again. We went to our rooms and everyone came to mine where (gasp, don't tell) we all had drinks. The stiff shot of vodka felt good as I looked out of the window at the rain that had begun again. I felt like a teenager in love when I thought about Jane being here tomorrow. After our cocktails, we ate dinner at a local restaurant that sold t-shirts printed with pictures of the last official hanging in the Panhandle.

We drove around Clarendon and looked at the sights, including a giant steel cross at the First Methodist Church and the museum that is located in what once had been a hospital. Then we returned to our rooms. After I went to sleep, I dreamed that I had a special harness and was pulling this huge wagon packed with Jane's clothes and possessions. I dreamed that I was walking up a hill but the wagon was not hard to pull at all.

Chapter Eleven

We walked into Clarendon
A town where sin has vanished
To help people stay good
Liquor has been banished.
Walk across Texas
With its wonderful sights.
Walk across Texas
With its beautiful nights.

Eddie announced at breakfast that we were two days behind schedule on our mileage chart. But, he did not seem too concerned. "We can walk a couple of twenty-mile days and go without taking a day off and we'll be back on our schedule," he said.

Norm had told us about seeing a friendly horse during his walk the day before. So we drove north of Clarendon to the site he had mentioned. We climbed from the car and Norm walked to the fence and began whistling. Soon we heard a horse whinnying and the sound of its hooves coming toward us. Then we saw a beautiful buckskin filly running to the fence. She stopped and Norm began petting and talking to her. Eddie and I joined him and she allowed us to pet her also.

"She's so pretty and friendly," said Norm.

We left and drove to my walking point. Eddie let me out and then drove to his and Norm's starting points. I walked about a mile and saw four mule deer standing near the side of the road. I walked to within thirty feet of them before they finally bolted and leaped, easily clearing the fence. They looked beautiful as they ran through the rugged pastureland.

I walked another two miles and Brad Shadle came riding up on a horse to say hello. He asked me if I was all right. I told him I was.

"I was getting ready to go out to the pasture and I saw you and I just wanted to make sure you didn't need anything," he said. He said he was breaking the horse he was riding. "He's still kinda skittish, but I think he'll make a good horse."

I asked about the filly we had seen north of us.

"Oh, yeah, I know her. I broke her about four years ago. She's a really nice pony," he said.

I told him about our walking across Texas.

"I think that is neat," he said. "You fellers are getting a good view of the country. You are seeing things that people driving down the highway

Norm Snyder made friends with this horse located in a pasture between Jayton and Pampa. Photos by Eddie Lane and Norm Snyder.

don't see. Take that canyon right across the road. I think that is one of the most beautiful sites around here."

He pointed to a ragged looking canyon that dug deep into the pasture-land, flatlands and hills revealing red clay with stone formations.

"That canyon goes all the way to Palo Duro. That's about fifty miles from here. If you got on a horse, you could ride it all the way in that canyon. But, it would be rough. It's so rough in places that there are maverick cattle in there that have never seen a man. I've heard that some of the old cows are so crazy, that when they are caught and put in a trailer they get so excited that they die before they can get them out of there. Now, that's something that only you'll see because you're walking."

He said he had lived on the Goodnight Ranch when he was a young-ster. "My daddy worked for old man Goodnight," he said.

We talked about some of the Goodnight history. His JA Ranch once covered some one million acres and occupied most of four counties in this area. His ranching life with his partner, Oliver Loving, was used by Larry McMurtry in his book, *Lonesome Dove*. And the book was made into a film that starred Robert Duvall as Loving and Tommie Lee Jones as Goodnight. The movie actually follows many of the events in the lives of Goodnight and Loving, including the time when they were driving cattle to sell at Fort Sumner, New Mexico. Loving and a cowboy left the herd and Goodnight to go ahead and check on the market at Fort Sumner. Indians attacked them and Loving was wounded during the battle and could not continue to ride. So the cowboy left Loving beside a river and walked eighty miles back to find Goodnight and to tell him about Loving's predicament. In the movie, that cowboy was known as Pea Eye. In real life his name was Billy Wilson. He had lost an arm in an accident early in his life and was known as One-Arm Billy Wilson. In my days at the *Fort Worth Star-Telegram,* I had been told about Wilson and was taken to his burial site in Palo Pinto County.

In the movie, as well as in real life, Goodnight rode to Fort Sumner where Loving died from his injuries. Goodnight promised that he would not leave his friend there, but would return and take his body back to Texas for burial. He did this, and I interviewed a man who claimed that his father had been in Weatherford when Goodnight arrived on the wagon with his friend's body in a casket, preserved by rock salt. Loving is buried in a Parker County cemetery.

Goodnight became known as one of Texas' famed ranching characters. He once rode bareback from Illinois to Texas when he was only nine years old. He was a Texas Ranger and is given credit for creating cattle trails from Texas to Denver and Kansas City covering nearly 2,000 miles. He became known as a great breeder of range cattle and an international authority on the cattle industry.

"He was one helluva cattleman and one helluva man," said Shadle. He pulled his hat off, shook it and put it back on his head. "I've got to check on my cattle. Next time you come through here, be sure and stop and say howdy. And, if you do this again, why don't you try riding a horse? Might be easier."

I continued walking and thought of another character who had once ridden in this area in the 1870s. His name was Sostenes L'Archevêque and he was considered by many to be one of the worst killers in the Southwest. He developed a hatred for Anglo-Americans after one killed his father. He pledged that he would kill every gringo he met after that. He killed twenty-three before Hispanic cowboys killed him. His last victims were two brothers named Casner. That triggered another set of brutal killings by the Casner family who vowed to kill every Mexican in the Panhandle. They killed several before finally settling in Donley County.

My thoughts changed to food when I reached the car about noon. I drove to Eddie and Norm. We decided to eat a picnic lunch of Vienna sausages, crackers, cheese, onions, fruit juice, and apples. After eating, we drove to Clarendon and looked at the Church of St. John the Baptist, the oldest Episcopal church continuously in use in the Texas Panhandle. Mrs. Elizabeth Goffat, a donor from Philadelphia, chose the name for the church that was consecrated in 1893. The white frame structure has a wooden shingle roof and a steeple with a cross.

We drove across the city's brick streets and looked again at the Adair Hospital that's been converted into a museum. The property is also the site of the annual Charles Goodnight Chuck Wagon Cook-Off held the last weekend in September. Then we decided to visit Roger A. Estlack, publisher and editor of the *Clarendon Chronicle,* the oldest newspaper in the Texas Panhandle.

He told about trying to find the first edition of the newspaper during activities honoring its founding. "Nobody had one," he said. "I even offered a $1,000 reward to anyone who found one and brought it to the newspaper."

That was unsuccessful. Then during the first week in October 2006, he got an email from Pennsylvania. The writer said he had acquired from an antique dealer a complete set of the newspaper's first year editions. Estlack quickly negotiated a price and bought the newspapers.

"People have asked us how the newspaper got to Pennsylvania. We think that maybe the first publisher may have sent them up there in order to encourage settlers to come to this country," said Estlack.

He showed us that first edition and told us some of the newspaper's early history. L.H. Carhart, who founded Clarendon, started the publication that was called *The Clarendon News.* The first paper was published June 1, 1878.

"The paper was a monthly," said Estlack. "He put it together here and then shipped it to Oshkosh, Wisconsin, to be printed. After printing, it was shipped back down here and sold. That's why it was a monthly."

The early edition did have a slant on religion since Carhart had founded the city as a Christian enclave. That showed in a poem in the first edition about a minister's wife. Part of it reads:

For thy will be worn and wearing.
Needing a change of life.
And, then we'll advertise.
Wanted: a minister and his wife.

Estlack said his family had owned the newspaper from 1929 until 1974 when they sold it. But, he and his wife, Ashlee, bought it back in 1995. And, no, he does not mind living in such a conservative town.

"Yes, we have a lot of churches for a town this size. But, there is something for everybody," he said. "Like we have the oldest Methodist, Episcopal, Catholic, and African American church in the Panhandle. Really, there is something for everyone."

Ashlee, his wife, and her sister, Anndria Kidd, agreed. Ashlee graduated from Clarendon High School. She said she liked driving down the street and seeing people she knew and being able to wave at them and get a wave in response. "I like being a somebody rather than a nobody," said

Ashlee, twenty-one. "I went to work for Roger when I was seventeen. I went to state in feature writing in high school. I also worked at the flower shop. But, Roger kept begging me to quit that and work here. So I did. But, I still do public relations for the college."

We said our good-byes and returned to the motel to await the arrival of Jane and Barbara. When I saw them turn onto the parking lot, I rushed outside to greet Jane with a hug and a kiss. She smelled so good.

"Have you boys been having fun?" asked Barbara.

"A little," I said. I smiled. "But, we will have more now that you are here."

After checking them into the motel, we met in our room. We all had a drink and Norm and I told about our experiences, including Norm's new friend, the horse. "We will have to drive you out there tomorrow and introduce you to her," he said.

We ate dinner and returned to the motel. We watched television and then went to sleep. I told Jane how good it was to feel her lying next to me. I knew that when she left, the next twenty days were going to be long ones.

Chapter Twelve

We woke up one morning
With frost nibbling our feet
Eddie said softly
Well, thank God it's not sleet.
Walk across Texas
With its wonderful sights.
Walk across Texas
With its beautiful nights.

Both Barbara and Jane questioned our decision to walk on their first day with us. A north wind hitting thirty miles an hour had sent the wind chill factor down to thirty-nine degrees. Eddie laughed at the suggestion that maybe we shouldn't walk.

"Layer up," he said. "Once you get started walking, you'll be okay."

So we layered and began our walk to Turkey. Eddie's advice proved to be right. After about thirty minutes, the cold didn't seem so bad. We walked five miles and then decided to drive to Turkey to eat lunch and look at the town, which once was called Turkey Roost because of the wild turkeys that roosted in trees along Turkey Creek. The town is also famed for being the home of the late Bob Wills, said by many to be "the father of western swing music." The town has erected a statue with a fiddle on top near the downtown area. Wills, who had lived on a cotton farm outside of Turkey, had learned to play the fiddle as a youngster. A plaque told of the lives of Wills and the Playboys.

"He and the Texas Playboys appeared in many motion pictures. Songs he (Wills) wrote and recorded with the Playboys included 'San Antonio Rose,' 'Spanish Two Step,' 'Maiden's Prayer,' 'Take Me Back to Tulsa,' 'Time Changes Everything,' and 'Ida Red,'" read the plaque.

The monument sits near a city park that is packed the last weekend of April every year during the annual Bob Wills Day Celebration. We looked at the park and then drove to Lacy's Dry Goods, an old-time department store owned by Hubert and Delores Price.

Paulette Lipscomb, a sales clerk, delighted us with stories about Turkey and the store. She said when cotton, once the king crop in this area, went on a decline, people started raising sweet potatoes and Turkey became well known for its sweet potatoes.

"And this store, well Delores is the third generation to own this store. You really don't see one like it any more," she said.

She pointed to the tables where jeans, shirts, bolts of fabric, spools of thread, and other items were stacked. "These are the original tables," she said. "You know, I think we're probably the only one like it that has this kind of diversified items. In other places like Childress and Plainview, customers have to go to a Wal-Mart."

The arrival of a male customer proved some of the uniqueness of Lacy's. He looked at Lipscomb and said, "I think you ordered some jeans for me a couple of days ago." As Lipscomb looked for the jeans, he turned to me and said, "This is a great place. If they don't have your size, they will order them and you'll get them in a couple of days."

Lipscomb filled the order and said the same thing applied to boots. "We've sold ropers so long from Justin Boots that if we don't have a size we just pick up the phone and call them and they send them to us. It's the same with the Wranglers (jeans)," she said.

We looked some more and then walked outside. The sandy brick building sat beside the Gem Theatre that was promoting the coming of Bryan Burline's Band. Ribbons of sand blown in from the nearby farming fields lined the parking spaces along the main street.

We drove to what had once been the local high school. It now houses the Bob Wills Museum, city hall, senior citizens center, Justice of the Peace, public library, and the Turkey Medical Clinic. We stepped into the museum and heard the Wills song, "Faded Love," playing in the background. A piano played by Al Stricklin during a stint at the White Elephant in Fort Worth sat in an exhibit case. The piano had been donated by Joseph K. Dulle and had been dedicated to Alton (Brother Al) Stricklin, Wills' original piano player. A book I wrote about Stricklin was in the display case.

We left the museum and drove to where we had stopped walking that morning. I began the first five-mile stretch. I walked past red clay banks and land covered with mesquite and sage. I looked into the hills and saw some coyotes sneaking under the mesquite limbs. They looked at me and then took off in a burst of speed, leaving only a brown streak. I kept walking and passed a sign that warned of "earth slides." I passed the Clear Fork of the Red River and came to the car where Jane was waiting. A herd of black cattle with white faces stood in the pasture looking at us. Jane rolled the window down and began saying, "Mooocow. Mooocow." The cattle looked at her and some started moving toward the fence.

"You should enter the cattle calling contest at Miami," I said.

We drove to Norm and Barbara and picked them up. They both were excited over the game they had seen during their walk.

"We saw mule deer and coyotes," said Barbara. "The deer were just absolutely beautiful."

We headed back to Clarendon. We passed a dead feral hog. Buzzards circled the carcass. About a mile further down the road, I pulled over. Orange ribbons of erosion lined the canyon, making a stunning view. We looked at a rock formation hanging onto the canyon walls that looked like an old castle that had been chiseled from the rock and into the ragged sides that sloped toward a dry creek bed.

"That is awesome," said Jane.

Our silence boomed an echo of agreement. We looked for several minutes and then drove back to Clarendon.

Chapter Thirteen

We walked past farmers
And cowboys working cattle
Sitting on their horses
Like they were dressed for battle.
Walk across Texas
With its wonderful sights.
Walk across Texas
With its beautiful nights.

We had coffee with Douglas and Martha Lowe in the motel lobby. They told us more stories about Clarendon and the area. He's a large, strong looking man and both of them are warm and friendly.

"You be sure and call us when and if you come back through here," he said.

Eddie had already packed and left for Caprock Canyon State Park where he would meet us later in the day. So we packed and headed for the campground. As we loaded our stuff into Barbara's car, I noticed that my hiking stick was gone. We unpacked the car and could not find it.

"I'll bet you left it where we stopped yesterday when we were walking," said Jane.

"Maybe it's still there," I said.

Everyone laughed at that possibility as we got into the car and headed for Turkey. We drove through some farmland and then countryside marked by long hills, river flats, and canyon walls. We reached the place where Jane and I had stopped. There, propped on a highway curve sign, was my hiking stick.

"That says something about the honesty of the people in this area," I said.

"Or it may say that the hiking stick you are carrying is not worth stealing," said Jane.

We continued to Turkey and decided to return to the community clinic to get flu shots. Dan Turner, a former Green Beret and physician's assistant, took our names and then administered the shots. I was impressed by how quickly he made the injections.

"A lot of people ask me why I'm so good at giving shots," he said. "I tell them I guess I learned from giving so many shots to horses. But, I learned from the horses, how to hold the skin and give the shot in a way that it doesn't bother the horse. You give a bad shot to a horse and he'll kick the snot out of you."

His prowess has so impressed an elderly woman that when she goes to a doctor and he says she needs some kind of shot, she tells him to fill up the syringe and let her take it to Turner so he can make the injection.

We thanked him and headed for Quitaque located about twenty miles northwest of Turkey. As we drove, I thought about Memphis, the seat of Hall County. It was a town without a name until the Rev. J.W. Brice was in Austin and happened to see a letter addressed by accident to Memphis, Texas, rather than Tennessee, with the notation "No such town in Texas." So he submitted the name Memphis and it was accepted. Another story about Memphis told about it having no train depot and as a result trains did not stop there. Residents took care of that situation by slicking up the train tracks with a liberal dousing of lye soap, causing the train's wheels to spin and eventually stop the locomotive.

Another colorful story is told about Gazelle a town that was located in south central Hall County. According to local legend, the post office there was discontinued in 1903 and a postmaster moved it to a new location that was inside his house. However, his son contacted smallpox and postal customers refused to come there for mail. Nobody would take over the post office because of a fear of catching smallpox. So the man finally had to fumigate the postal fixtures and return them to postal authorities in Washington.

We reached Quitaque on Highway 86 where we ate lunch. The town is small with several empty buildings on downtown streets. The first settler here was a Comanchero trader who operated a trading post from 1865 to 1867, trading dry goods and ammunition to the Comanches for stolen livestock. Colonel Charles Goodnight, the rancher, thought that the name Quitaque meant end of the trail. Another story said it came from two buttes in the area that resembled piles of horse manure, the real meaning of the Indian word. Still another story says that the name came from the Quitaca Indians, whose name was translated by white settlers as "whatever one steals."

After lunch, we drove to Caprock Canyons State Park three miles north of Quitaque. The park is the third largest in Texas and has some 13,960 acres of rough terrain. Landscapes are carved by erosion at the edge of the caprock, forming colorful cliffs and canyons where wildlife includes mule and white-tailed deer and imported North African aoudad sheep. One of the park's most interesting features is the Folsom site near Lake Theo, one of five such sites in the nation. Several Folsom points and the remains of an extinct Ice Age bison have been found there, giving substantial evidence that Folsom man manufactured and made use of his weapons here about 10,000 years ago.

Eddie greeted us. He had picked a nice campsite and already had the Highway Hilton assembled and ready for sleeping. We said our good-byes

This mountain range lies in the Caprock Canyon State Park near Quitaque. Photos by Eddie Lane and Norm Snyder.

to Barb and Jane and watched the taillights of their car fade into the distance. I admit that I felt a little depressed.

Eddie soon chased away my depression when he announced, "We got several hours left. Let's go walk."

So we drove to our stopping point of the day before and began our five-mile increments with a ten-mile-per-hour north wind at our backs. The temperature was in the mid-fifties, which made for pleasant walking.

Freshly plowed wheat fields lay to the side of the road. Mounds of sunflowers with bright yellow blossoms stood beside the road. The farmlands emitted a strong, fresh, raw, and pleasant smell.

After walking five miles, I reached the car and drove to pick up Norm and Eddie. We returned to Caprock Park where we stopped and looked at a copy of the next day's weather forecast that called for colder temperatures and rain. We decided that we would stay one night and then leave.

I wandered around the camping area as Eddie cooked our dinner. I had camped here many times and always felt like it is one of our state's better facilities. I recalled one night I had camped here with David Bickley, my brother-in-law. We had arrived after six P.M. and had several drinks after cooking dinner. I was relating some story and I am prone to get a little loud in my storytelling when I have been reinforced with scotch. Two women camped in the next camping site suddenly shouted, "Hey, we don't find that story nearly as interesting as your friend does. Will you tone it down some?"

I walked back to our camping site. Eddie had cooked chicken and dumplings, made with flour tortillas. They were delicious. We also had huge pieces of canned fruit. I looked at Eddie and said, "Hey, you are really replenishing our calories tonight." I had tuned the radio to a station that played rock from the fifties. One of the songs was "Help me information, get in touch with my Marie. The last time that I saw her, was in Memphis, Tennessee." Old memories of my high school days and more simple times came flooding back to my mind.

"Hey, guess what?" said Eddie.

"What?" I asked.

"We are a third of the way home," he said.

"Really?" asked Norm.

"Really," he said.

That gave me a boost. I thought of what that actually meant. We had walked 150 miles. That was a bunch for anyone. The way I felt that night, I knew that I could make it the rest of the way without any trouble. I looked at my walking buddies. I thought, "And, we've come this far and haven't had any major argument or confrontation."

The north wind had gotten stronger and the cold bit into our camping site. I put on a heavy cotton sweater and then pulled a coat on over that. I still felt a little cold. I watched the stars flick in and out of skinny films of clouds floating by. I looked deep into the sky and could see many of the constellations like the Seven Sisters, the Great Hunter, and the Big and Little Dippers. As I looked at the beautiful formations, the coyotes began their crazy off key singing. I thought, "Does it get any better than this?"

Eddie had built a campfire. I walked over to it, turned around and felt its warmth eat into my hips and back. The wood smoke smelled wonderful. I looked up at the stars again and then headed for the Highway Hilton and my bed. Aw, what a life.

Chapter Fourteen

We saw many deer
Bounding past us with antlers
They jumped over fences
Looking like ballet dancers.
Walk across Texas
With its wonderful sights.
Walk across Texas
With its beautiful nights.

Heavy dew soaked into the ends of my sleeping bag after a tarp stretched over the bag pulled out. I felt the cold and wetness and tried to scoot my feet to a dry side but when I got warm and relaxed my feet seemed to slip back into the wetness. I kicked the sleeping bag off and quickly put on my sweat pants and sweatshirt before stumbling outside.

The smells of bacon cooking in a skillet greeted me. Eddie also had a pot of coffee ready and it tasted delicious despite it burning my throat as I swallowed. It felt good chasing away some of the early morning cold.

We decided after reviewing the weather forecast of colder temperatures and more rain that we would stick with our earlier decision to pack up and move camp on down the road and try to find a motel in Matador for the night. As I drank more coffee I looked at the sunrise with its striking red streaks entwined with flashes of grays and dark blues. We completed our packing and headed for Quitaque where we stopped at Karol's Kountry Korner, a gift, flower, and collectibles shop.

The shop is inside a red and white painted building that once had been an old Mobil station. Outside are several aging soft drink advertisements for Royal Crown Cola, Dr Pepper, and Ted's Creamy Root Beer, a soft drink made in honor of the late great baseball player Ted Williams. A manual gasoline pump sat outside. It had a glass container with gallons indicated on the inside with numbers. We walked inside and met Karol Pigg, owner.

"This used to be my grandfather's grocery and service station," she said. "He ran a little mom and pop operation here for better than fifty years. His name was J.D. Blankenship and everybody called him Mister Blankenship."

She remembered helping at the store when she was a little girl. She would scoop out beans from a container built especially for beans, weigh them, and tell the customer how much they cost. She said she graduated from Quitaque High School and remembered the Midway Drive-in Theater that we had passed earlier.

"Oh, yeah, I certainly remember the Midway," she said. "Everybody went to it, and we'd park on the back row and have a good time watching the movie."

She said she was a bookkeeper for a cotton gin company for fifteen years before buying the old store. "I love it," she said. "It's not like I have to go to work every day. It's, well, it's fun."

We bid our good-byes and drove to our starting point for the walk to Matador, some twenty-eight miles away. We had walked fourteen of those miles yesterday and figured that we would not have any trouble reaching the town today.

Matador is the seat of Motley County, a sparsely settled territory with 959 square miles of rough and broken terrain. The land is drained by the North Pease, Middle Pease, and South Pease rivers. Their tributaries include Dutchman, Bear, Torn Handle, South Canyon, Sand, Chief Hollow, Shinnery Draw, Fish, and Turtle Hole creeks.

The county was organized in 1891 and required some unusual work by the giant Matador Land and Cattle Company. The General Land Office of Texas required a county seat to have at least twenty businesses. Matador did not have that number so the Matador Ranch had employees open temporary stores and stocked them with ranch supplies to meet the requirements.

By the mid-1980s, Motley was one of sixty-two Texas counties that were still legally dry. But, the small city had once been a rather wild place when the DewDrop Saloon operated until 1893, when prohibition was voted in. Some people claim that helped the community become a peaceful place that did not have its first bank robbery until 1966.

Our walk carried us along a highway bordered by grain fields and grasslands with cattle grazing on grass growing in the red clay, sandy, and black soils located just below the Caprock. We passed fencerows that had been covered by sand and had new fences built on top of them. Huge gas tanks containing fuel for farm equipment dotted the countryside. I looked at tractors with air-conditioned cabs and fancy stereo systems, a far cry from the old tractors with steel seats that my brother and I once used.

We walked past fields with crops of sudan and pastures with thousands of mesquites. Massive bunches of sage grew along the North Pease River, a tiny stream of water that looked like somebody had dumped a bucket of red paint into it. The South Pease River flows in the southwestern part of the county and is also called the Tongue River. The stream got that name because of the black tongue, a nineteenth-century disease that killed many buffalo in the region.

Just north of Matador, we met Jim Meadow, Motley County sheriff for fifteen years. He's a tall, strongly built man. His wife owns *The Motley County Tribune* and he wanted to take a picture of us for the newspaper. He

Wild hogs run plentiful in the Texas Panhandle and are bought for meat at hog buying stations like this one, located north of Jayton. This photo shows some of the wild hogs that had just been unloaded from a trailer. Photos by Eddie Lane and Norm Snyder.

parked his pick-up truck and talked about the history of the county and other things. I asked him about the wild hogs.

"Aw, we got a bunch of them," he said. "Attack a person? I doubt it unless you got between one of them old sows and her piglets and she thought you were going to hurt her piglets. She might attack you then and if she wanted to catch you, there is no way you could outrun her on foot."

He said he had tried eating the meat but did not like it. "Somebody shoot one of them old boars, I wouldn't give you a nickel for it. They might as well drop him off the canyon wall, as far as I'm concerned," he said.

I asked him about the late Dr. Albert Carroll Traweek, who once made house calls in the county on a motorcycle. One call he made involved a woman rancher whose stomach was ripped open by the horns of a bull. Her intestines had fallen out and she had picked them up and held them with her apron until Dr. Traweek arrived. He cleaned the intestines, put them back inside her stomach, and then sutured the wound closed. She recovered.

"Yeah, I knew him," said Meadow. "He's the man who brought me into the world. He was quite a doctor. That story doesn't surprise me a bit. I used to go in for a shot and he would take the syringe and needle out of this bottle of alcohol. He would squirt a little of that alcohol out and then give you a shot. That would be unheard of today."

We asked him about another landmark known as Bob's Oil Well. He smiled.

"Yeah, I also knew old Bob. He was a promoter. Built this oil derrick over his filling station and then gave out brochures telling about his station to truckers and asked them to post them all over the country. He got a lot of business that way," he said. "Be sure and stop at the old filling station. It's got a historical marker."

So we drove on into Matador and stopped at Bob's Oil Well. You can't miss the site. Just go until you see this hundred-or so-foot steel oil well derrick sticking up over an abandoned filling station. A marker tells about Luther Bedford (Bob) Robertson, a Greenville native, World War I veteran, and businessman who came here in the 1920s to work as a gas station attendant.

He opened his own station in 1932 and decided to build a wooden oil well derrick over it in order to promote business. He replaced that with a steel derrick that included lights. Then he wrote a brochure noting the mileage to Bob's Oil Well and paid long distance truck drivers to take them and pass them out across the nation. In the meantime, he opened a zoo at the station that included a pit of rattlesnakes, monkeys, coyotes, and a white buffalo. Business grew. So he opened a grocery, café, and garage.

He died in 1947 and two weeks after his death, a high wind toppled his steel derrick. But, his widow, Olga, restored it. She eventually sold the enterprise and it closed in the 1950s. Efforts to reopen it were not successful.

"Today, the site serves as a reminder of a time when such bold roadside architecture was in its infancy and of a man who, through his business, widely promoted his adopted town," reads the marker.

The three of us backed off and looked at the site that sits at the intersection of Highway 60 and Highway 72. We all agreed that it was impressive.

We drove to downtown Matador with its wide, brick paved streets. We ate lunch at the Main Street Café and listened to people express thanks for the recent and continuing rain. We walked outside and a thick mist coated our car's windshield. Since it was still early afternoon, we drove on to Dickens, crossing the South Pease River and entering Dickens County.

The rain continued, blotting out the heavy growth of mesquites. We looked at the rain and the countryside and Eddie said, "Let's call this a rest afternoon and see what we can find to stay in at Dickens."

"Barbara said that Dickens is supposed to be the wild boar capital of Texas," said Norm. "Maybe you can find somebody to talk to about that."

As we drove through the rain, I remembered another bit of history of Motley County I read concerning a train line that operated out of Matador in 1914. An engineer made a passenger carrier called a Jigger that had been built from a Model T Ford truck rigged to run on the rails. I bet it made

The late Bob Robertson built this oil well derrick over his filling station in Matador in the 1930s to attract business. He also had a small zoo at the location, and people from all over the United States came here for a visit until the station closed in the 1950s after Robertson's death. Photos by Eddie Lane and Norm Snyder.

quite a sight when it roared down the railway in rain like we were driving through.

The late Elizabeth Bundy Campbell, wife of Henry H. Campbell, one of the founders of the famed Matador Ranch, discovered another unusual Motley County landmark, a hill covered with petrified wood. When she arrived in the country from Fort Worth, she slept in a tent because she refused to sleep in a dugout that her husband had used for a year. She was one of only two women living in the area at the time and the other woman lived some twenty miles away.

She became famous for large Christmas parties she gave every year. The parties lasted for two or three days and she stacked her home-cooked food on tables. She loved ranching and riding and often rode her horse by herself across the thousands of acres of the ranch. It was during one of those rides that she discovered a hill covered with petrified wood that eventually became known on maps as "Mrs. Campbell's Petrified Hill."

I looked across the countryside and thought of Mrs. Campbell and the other early residents who came to carve out a living from this raw, rugged land. Learning about these people and talking to their descendants made walking all of these miles worthwhile.

Chapter Fifteen

We ate every thing offered
Burgers, tacos even prickly pear
After consuming that delicacy
Norm said, "I'll eat anywhere."
Walk across Texas
With its wonderful sights.
Walk across Texas
With its beautiful nights.

The evidence of rain lay everywhere as we began our thirteenth day on the road. Water stood between the rows of cotton as we drove down the highway. There also were more of the playa lakes filling shallow places in the land, reminding one of when grandma emptied her dishpan onto the soil outside her back porch.

We drove to the site of Anderson's Fort, also known as Soldier's Mound, which is six miles south of Dickens in south central Dickens County. The mound stretched to some 2,488 feet in width in the 1870s and became known as Anderson's Fort after Major Thomas M. Anderson occupied the site and fortified it with sandbags and rock walls. It later was called Lawton's Supply Camp, and Colonel Ranald S. Mackenzie used the mound as a supply point during his campaign in the 1870s to force the Comanche Indians from this territory onto the reservation.

The ridge became known as Soldier's Mound because it was the burial site for several soldiers and Indians. The hill was also the site of a buffalo hunters' camp and in 1878 the Spur Ranch located its headquarters nearby. We parked our car, got out, and looked at the mound that looks like a large loaf of bread. An oil well pump slowly went up and down in the foreground as we looked. A gray and heavy blanket of clouds hung over the site. Bales of hay dotted the countryside slightly to the west.

We returned to the car and drove to Spur to look at our next walk-through site. We stopped at the Backdoor Inn, a café inside an old filling station. On this morning it was filled with coffee drinkers talking about the blessings of the five inches of rain that had fallen. Eddie told the men about our walk. One asked how old he was.

"Seventy-seven," he said.

"Well, I'm only sixty-five but I got more miles on me than you do," said the man.

I had heard many references to the Croton Brakes, supposedly a really rough portion of country in this area. One story I heard said that if cattle got lost in the brakes they would not be found until ten years later. I asked the men if this were true and where we could look at the brakes.

"Yeah, that's probably true about cattle," said one man. "I know the brakes are rough to ride a horse in. So if you were thinking about walking in them, well, you'd better think about that again. They are as rough as an old boot that's been lined with barbed wire."

We told him that we had no desire to walk in the Croton Brakes. We just wanted to find out where they were so we could go look at them. He gave us directions, leaned back in his chair and said, "You boys be careful when you go to them old brakes. There's rattlesnakes and gawd knows what else crawling around in them."

We thanked them and drove back through Dickens and headed east of town on Highway 116. A gray fog had moved into the area and hung thickly over the ground. We stopped after a few miles and looked at what we thought were the Croton Brakes, a raw, ragged chunk of land with junipers, mesquites, and a series of rough canyons that had been gouged out of the red clay soils. The fog dipped lower like a soiled bed sheet and I thought, "Yeah, I would not want to be out in those messing around." I also felt like I knew why locals referred to the Croton Brakes in almost personal tones.

Actually, the Croton Brakes cover about a 250-square mile area below the escarpment of the Llano Estacado. The brakes are severely eroded, marked with densely dissected gullies and low hills, typical badlands topography with shallow topsoil, or none. Stories of lost mines full of riches in the brakes frequently have been told. But, so far nobody has discovered any of these mines.

One of the early settlers of this area was Mrs. Arrie Ella Elgar Dumont, a well-known sculptor and seamstress. She created beautiful buckskin gloves, vests and pants. Her first husband, James Thomas Bird, was a Texas Ranger and line camp rider for the well-known Pitchfork Ranch. She began sculpting and once paid a doctor bill with a sculptured napkin ring decorated with flowers and topped by a squirrel holding an acorn. After the death of her first husband, she carved a five-foot high tombstone of a model church building filled with flowers. She also sculpted a bible as an heirloom for her children. Unfortunately, her sculptures were either stolen or destroyed by a storm at the family home near Paducah in 1895.

We drove back to Dickens and looked at the beautiful sandstone courthouse that had an old wood framed windmill sitting on the lawn. A sign said the windmill had been purchased at the Riter Hardware Store in Spur and installed on the A.J. Slaton Farm in 1927. It had been moved to the Dickens Courthouse Square in April 1999. I looked at the old windmill and its blades and thought of the history those blades could tell if there were some way of unwinding them and listening to their stories. One of the well-known windmills in Dickens County was called the Poison because an early settler had tried to poison a cowboy by poisoning the water his windmill pulled from the ground.

Another nearby marker told about Sheriff W.B. "Bill" Arthur, who was known by adults and children as Bill. He was shot and killed during a jail-break on October 25, 1934. High school boys served as his pallbearers.

We left Dickens and drove to Roaring Springs, located fifteen miles north on Highway 70. We looked at the old depot that is being restored. An ancient fire truck sat parked near one end. Nearby, an aging homemade catamaran sailboat sat on a four-wheel farm trailer. Paint crumbled off its sides, and the sails were shredded and torn. The pontoons were painted blue and white.

"I hate to see something like that so deteriorated," said Eddie. "Somebody's dream is being dissolved by time."

A license tag on the trailer read May 1992.

We were silent as we climbed back into the car and drove back to the motel. Rain had started again and soaked us as we ran from the car to our rooms. We turned on the weather channel and heard that flash floods, tornadoes, and colder weather had been forecast for the rest of the day and tomorrow.

"It's not supposed to ever rain out here, is it?" asked Norm.

We moved into my room for a drink and watched the rest of the Dallas Cowboys game. Eddie used the time to repair a pair of his shorts that he had ripped. He had no needle or thread. No problem—duct tape. As he worked, we talked about the research we had done on our book about the bridges over the Brazos River. We talked about visiting my late son Patrick in Bryan and how he had arranged for us to see La Bella, the boat sailed by the French explorer La Salle when he had visited the Texas coast. The ship had been found buried in the sand in waters off the shores of the gulf.

"Patrick would love this trip," I said. "He likes Texas history so much and you know he is researching a book about the early gangsters and the effect they had on the early oil boomtowns in Texas."

I stopped. I realized that I was referring to Patrick in the present tense as if he were still alive. I looked at Eddie and Norm. They both remained silent. Patrick had died in 2005.

We watched the end of the game and decided to eat barbecue in a convenience store barbecue place. We walked inside and sat at the one and only heavy wooden table with brands burned deeply in the top. The only chairs were around this table.

"If there are any more customers, we'll get to know them, well," said Eddie.

A fly swatter lay on the table. Horseshoes were nailed into the serving counter's walls. The smell of meat cooking was tantalizing. After eating we returned to our rooms. Outside, the rain continued to fall in heavy sheets. We watched it hammer against our windows.

"Norm, you are absolutely right," said Eddie. "It is not supposed to rain this way in this part of the country."

So much for trying to predict Texas weather. We poured ourselves another drink and sat silently for several minutes. Then Norm and Eddie said they had made a remarkable discovery during our walk. They both had been counting the number of empty beer cans they spotted along the roadside.

"What did your survey reveal?" asked Eddie.

"That beer drinkers in this area prefer Bud Lite by about three to one," said Norm.

Eddie smiled. "I found the same thing. Before I started counting, I figured that Coors Lite would be the preferred beer," he said. "Of course, you realize that this is a strictly nonscientific survey."

I said that it proved something else.

"What?" they both asked at the same time.

"That the things we do to entertain ourselves while walking sometimes reach the ridiculous," I said.

We all laughed and said our goodnights.

Chapter Sixteen

We talked to many people
Who told all kinds of tales
Like the one about the Croton Breaks
That looks like a page torn from hell.
Walk across Texas
With its wonderful sights.
Walk across Texas
With its beautiful nights.

Everybody talked about the rain the next morning and throughout the day. Of course, this country, like much of Texas had been in a drought that had parched the countryside for months. But, anytime rain comes in this part of Texas, it generates conversation.

We heard many stories as we ate our breakfast. The waitress had beautiful long black hair and wore jeans. She told about somebody getting stuck in his front yard and calling his friend Jerry for help.

"And, he goes over there in that big old pickup he has and damned if he didn't get stuck, too," she said. She roared with laughter, as did the other customers. Shortly afterwards Jerry walked into the café. He wore shredded jeans and a thick covering of mud came up almost past the tops of his shoes. His arms were muscled and he had wrists as thick as the big part of a baseball bat. Mud had splattered over his truck. He filled his coffee cup and began talking about the incident.

"Yeah, I pulled up in that front yard and hooked onto old Bobby's truck and began pulling. Damned if my truck didn't sink all the way down to the axles. So we had to call us a wrecker and he parked about twenty feet away from that front yard and hooked onto me and finally yanked me out," he said. "But, I tell you, we really got a good rain."

We finished our breakfast and since the rain had stopped, we began our walk toward Spur, which lay eleven miles south. Streams of water wider than we had seen yesterday lapped in the rows of cotton. Eddie also pointed out that there were even more of the playa lakes than there were yesterday. Orange-colored water ran in the bar ditches and warning signs about possible high water had been stationed along the highway.

We kept walking toward Spur. Judy Alter had emailed us that a delegation from Spur wanted to welcome us to their city so we looked forward to meeting those folks in that town of about 1,700.

We walked into Spur and stopped at a café called the Dixie Dog. Norm looked at it, grinned, and said, "I'll bet you could get a good hot dog there."

Then Joyce Howze, a strong looking friendly woman who is Spur Main Street Manager, arrived. She smiled, laughed, shook our hands, and welcomed us to her city. "I can't believe you guys are walking across Texas," she said. "When we read about your venture, we knew we had to show you Spur. We've got lots of things to see. Like we have an agricultural experiment station that was built here and they developed the syrup pan form of terracing for farming land. It provides full use of the rainfall and diverts water in such a way that it vastly improves crop yields. And, it is still being used across the country."

She said she was not a Spur native. "No sir, I am a Tennessee gal. I moved to Austin to work for Texas Parks and Wildlife in 1991. Then two years ago, we came to Spur," she said. "This is an interesting town and you don't know that unless you stop and smell the roses. Like, most of the homes in this town were built more than 100 years ago. And all of the buildings along Main Street were built around 1911."

I asked her if moving from Austin to Spur in this sparsely settled part of the Texas Panhandle was a cultural shock. She laughed. "Oh, no. We love it here. The peace and quiet and the people, well this is a nice place," she said.

We got a nice slice of the local people and the area's history for the next few hours as Howze led us on a tour of the city that included a stop at the old agricultural experiment station that is now closed. We looked at vacant buildings that had once been the office and home for the station's superintendent. The home had columns and a fence made from petrified wood. I could imagine how thrilled my friend Mary Saltarelli, who had done a study of the petrified wood buildings in Somervell County for her master's thesis, would be over seeing these creations. "We hope to get these buildings restored," said Howze.

Then we drove to the downtown area and stopped at Memory Lane Gift Shop, a building constructed in 1917 that once housed the local library. We went inside where Howze's husband, David, had brought barbecue brisket and the trimmings for lunch. "Hunting is our number one industry," said Howze. "That's next to cotton and ranching, of course."

Patti Sayers, president of the Spur Chamber of Commerce, and her husband, Richard, greeted us. They have lived here two years and love it. Richard wore jeans, boots, and a straw hat, and looked like he knew something about ranching. Eddie told him about seeing some wild hogs while walking.

"They looked like a train going across the road, didn't they," said Richard. He shook his head. "I've seen them many times going across the country and the way they were strung out they looked like a little ole train."

He told an interesting story about being attacked by a javelina while he was working on a ranch near Alpine. He had roped the javelina and had gotten off his horse to try to tie the animal. The hog charged him and somehow they became entwined with each other.

"He bit me on the knee and broke his tooth off and left it there," said Richard. "I wound up having to go to the hospital for a week. From then on people called me the hog fighter. But, I was zero to one in matches because that hog certainly got the best of me."

Somebody announced that lunch was ready. As we ate, we talked to Jim and Jewell Holder, owners of the Spur Inn and Holder's Guest House. She was reared five miles north of Dickens and said she used to play in the Croton Brakes. "They are a wild place but as a little girl I never thought anything about going on a hike in them," she said. "But, back before I was born, they said the Comanches and other Indians lived in the brakes."

Kenneth Gilcrease, mayor of Spur, a tall, lanky man who moved back here after working as a salesperson for forty years, told an Indian story. "My great-great grandmother was the first person to comb Cynthia Ann Parker's hair after they took her back from the Comanches," he said. "Her name was Sarah Curry Noland and she did that in Parker County." The Comanches had kidnapped Cynthia Ann Parker when she was a small child and she had lived with them for years, eventually marrying a Comanche before being returned to her family.

Henry Johns, eighty-four, who has lived in Spur since 1927, listened to the stories and then told about his life of exploring the countryside in the area. "I've walked all of the canyons around here pretty good," he said. "Yes sir, I have. I became really interested in the area's geology and the gypsum beds in Dickens County. And, I found some mica that was so clear you could read a newspaper through it."

The Sayerses invited us to come for a look at their home they are refurbishing. It was built between 1910 and 1920. After we arrived, she fixed coffee and he told about working on the Pitchfork Ranch, which covers 168,000 acres and is known for its three-pronged brand resembling a pitchfork.

"I heard you talking about the Croton Brakes. I worked in them brakes for eleven years. And, when Patti and I got married, I moved her to a place on the ranch called the Croton Camp. It was right on the edge of the brakes. We had no telephone, no TV reception, and our drinking water was water that ran off our roof and into a cistern."

After visiting the Sayerses, we went to the local museum and met Revvi Neaves, a slender, talkative, delightful woman who was born and reared in this area. She said she still runs a ranch and has eighty head of cattle. She was full of information about each exhibit and pointed at an old saddle, which she said was found in a cave in Soldier's Mound just north of Spur. "And, here we've got a headdress that Quanah Parker (he was Cynthia Ann

Parker's son) wore to Washington when Teddy Roosevelt was president," she said. "This is our prized possession. It is very rare."

The museum has such rare things that the Peabody Museum in Washington once called and offered to trade some whalebone for some dinosaur bones that had been collected in this area. "Not to be tacky, but we told them that we were not interested in a whale bone from the east," she said. "What would we do with one of those in our museum?"

We had stopped at a woman's sidesaddle, which was once used by women for horseback riding. I asked if she had ever ridden one of those. "Goodness, no," she said. "I never rode any kind of saddle. I never saw any need to. I look at my cattle practically every day but I do it from my pickup."

Andi Taylor, owner of the *Texas Spur,* the local newspaper, arrived and asked if she could take our photograph. "You men are famous," she said. "Walking all of that way and stopping here at Spur."

She said she was born here and at one time had left and worked in the corporate world. She sold expensive perfumes and women's accessories. The competition was fierce. "It was very superficial. The people were superficial. Everybody was out to cut your throat before you cut theirs," she said. She paused and thought a moment. She has rusty colored hair and blue eyes. "I wanted to control my own destiny and I figured the only way to do that was to buy my own business," she said. "Since I had grown up here, I thought why not come back. So I bought the newspaper ten years ago and haven't regretted it for a minute."

We left our hosts about three P.M. and decided to continue our walk toward Jayton, which was twenty-five miles away. The sights of the grain along our route and how it had become a vibrant green after the rain amazed me. I walked about two miles and stopped at a roadside park. Two county workers taking a break from mowing the park sat at the only table. They invited me to sit with them.

"We'd offer you a drink of water but we don't have any more," said one.

They told me they had been born and reared in this area and had been friends all of their lives. Both said they knew if they ever needed anything, that the other friend would be the first person they would call. "My daddy told me that you can really tell who your friends are when you run out of money to buy beer and cigarettes and your friend gives you the money," said one of the men.

I laughed and told them about a saying I had heard from a man in Granbury. "He said the two best sounds in the world that a man could hear was the sound of bacon frying in a skillet or money jingling in your pocket," I said.

We all laughed. Then they told about working in the cotton fields when people picked cotton by hand and dragged long canvas bags down the rows. "My mother used to pick cotton all day long. And, this was when my brother and me were just babies. She'd tie me and my brother onto her cotton sack and drag it and us down the cotton row, picking cotton," he said. He shook his head. "She'd do that until eleven-thirty in the morning. Then she would go to the house and cook a full meal for the family. After that she would go back to the cotton fields, tie my brother and me onto her sack, and continue picking cotton until about six or six-thirty that afternoon."

I sipped water from a bottle I had in my backpack. I told them about our walk. They finished their drinks and cigarettes and stood up. "Well, we got to get back to work," one of them said. "It's good talking to you. You boys be careful and we wish you the best on the rest of your walk."

I watched them leave and then got up and continued my walk toward the car, some three miles away. White packages of clouds hung in the sky. The wind had become stiff, but it was from the north so it made walking fairly easy. I thought of all that had happened to us today. I remembered something that Joyce Howze had said about stopping and smelling the roses. Walking certainly allowed a person to do that and made the distance we had to cover easier to accept. I kept walking toward the car.

Chapter Seventeen

We saw ragged canyons
Gouging through the land
And yet natives called them
Pages from the promise land
Walk across Texas
With its wonderful sights.
Walk across Texas
With its beautiful nights.

We found Putoff Canyon on our walk to Jayton. It is named for a Mister Putoff, an early settler in the area, and was once noted for its freshwater springs that flowed strong enough to swim a horse.

Many famous people visited a resort that existed in this rugged canyon. Those included author Zane Grey who became so intrigued with the area that he made it the location of *The Thundering Herd,* one of the many western novels he penned. We looked at the historical marker at the scene and then I walked through some brush to the edge of the canyon and looked at the dark red clay banks of gullies eating into the canyon walls. Mesquite, schinery, and cedars covered the ragged steep sides of the canyon. One hillside had quilt-like coverings of prickly pear, juniper, and mustard grass with brilliant yellow blossoms. Huge clumps of Spanish Daggers that looked like an old-time weapon of steel spikes grew in abundance.

I stepped back and looked down the canyons until they became blurry. I thought, "Yeah, I can see why Zane Grey and other authors would have been turned on so much by this area that they would use it as a setting for a book."

We drove back to our marked sections and began walking the last few miles to Jayton. Eddie met Seth Clay, a rancher who had a dog named Lizzie. Eddie said the dog had been crippled by an injury but still worked cattle for Clay who said, "She's the best dog I got."

Eddie asked him about all of the warnings we had received about wild hogs in the area. Clay warned about the wild sows, saying, "You corner one of the old sows on a bridge and she's got pigs, well it becomes a matter of how fast you can run. She will get you if you don't get some jets on your feet."

We walked on into Jayton, a small town once called Jay Flat and named after the Jay family, early ranchers in the area. We spotted the First National Bank and walked inside for a look at this historic structure established in 1907 by Kent County pioneers. The bank originally operated out of the Garnett Hotel before the directors decided to construct a building in 1912.

During a series of various owners the building was once designated as the Kent County courthouse for eighteen months. In 1962, Kent County State Bank was established and a new bank building was built beside the original structure that became a storage facility. In 1995, Kent County State Bank decided to renovate the old building, an example of early twentieth-century Classical Revival style. The results are impressive. The original teller stations constructed of oak with metal grills and beaded stained glass were restored. Also restored was the entrance with its leaded glass and oak framing.

The restoration crew discovered that the dome had been covered over with gold paint. The paint was removed, revealing a beautiful stained glass creation. Christy Hall, a bank employee and a Jayton native, told about some of the restoration. She said she attended kindergarten here and had moved to Haskell, never dreaming she would return. But, those dreams changed when she married Jay Hall, whose grandfather was the first CEO of the bank. She showed us some of the changes that had been made.

"That elk head (she pointed to a huge, stuffed elk head), it was one of the original wall decorations. They found it in a barn behind the house I lived in and brought it back to the bank," she said. "And, these paintings, they were originals. A man traveling though the country stopped and did those. Originally somebody wanted to paint over them."

The oil paintings are mountain scenes and are huge. She led us into the office of Bob E. Hamilton, a member of the board of directors and acting CEO and president. "I was born about two blocks east of here and my wife was born about two blocks north of here. That is about as native as you can get," he said.

As he talked about the bank's history, he chewed tobacco and held a paper cup in his hands that he used for a spittoon. He said he had an insurance agency that was located in front of the building for forty-five years. He said the restoration project faced some huge challenges. "One whole quarter of the ceiling had fallen in," he said. "And, the stained glass dome had been painted over with gold leaf to shut the sun out. They did that because of the heat. That was done in the days before air conditioning. Those paintings that Christy told you about . . . the architect wanted to paint over them. I said, no, no. This is a part of the bank. There was an old hotel across the street and this feller came to visit the people who owned that hotel. He was a painter so they hired him to paint those scenes."

He told about discovering an old black metal box that had been inside the bank vault for years. "Nobody ever looked into it because nobody had ever come in and asked for it," he said. "Finally, one day, somebody decided that we ought to see what was inside. Here let me show you what we found."

He showed us a photograph taken in 1899 of a building that looked like an old barn. Somebody had written on a piece of paper attached to the photograph, "House of where us lived in the brakes." The house had a roof that looked like it had been made from stacks of brush.

We returned to Hamilton's office and he began telling stories about the town and its residents. One was about his uncle who had an airplane that he loved to fly low through the canyons. "Everybody just knew he was going to crash and kill himself," said Hamilton. "But, he raised sheep, so coyotes were his worst enemy. So he carried a shotgun with him in the airplane and would shoot them as he flew along the canyons."

I asked him about the wild hogs in the area and if he felt like they would attack a human. "I don't know about that but I will tell you the durndest story about wild hogs. This trucker hit a bunch of them going across the road. He killed seven or eight of the hogs but he tore his truck all to pieces. It was just like hitting a bunch of rocks."

Then he told one last story about a man named Sleepy Browning. "He had kind of drooping eyelids," he said. "He had a barber shop and he loved to call square dancing. He went to England and Germany to call square dancing. Then he'd come back and barber. He had kind of a tremor in his hands. He'd come at you with his razor for a shave and it would make you quiver. But, right before he got to your face, he'd steady out and then he'd give you the smoothest shave possible. Never heard of him cutting anybody."

We said our good-byes, drove to where we had stopped and began walking again. We crossed the Salt Fork of the Brazos that was running almost full this day because of the recent rains. Eddie said it would be good for canoeing. We looked and smelled the fresh scent of the willows and mesquites that were heavy with beans. Sun splashed onto the beans and made them look like gold string hanging from limbs.

The dirty red water roared down the banks of the river and a huge limb that had been ripped from a tree came spiraling down. It crashed into a rock and made a cracking sound that echoed loudly along the riverbanks. We watched for about fifteen minutes and then we walked back to the car. Our mileage had been reached for the day, so we decided to make a side trip to Clairemont, a ghost town I had discovered about fifteen years earlier while I was writing my column for the *Fort Worth Star-Telegram*.

We drove to where Highway 208 cuts into Highway 70. Then we drove south to Clairemont, which had once been the seat of Kent County. A visit to the once thriving town is well worth the effort if for no other reason than to see the abandoned two-story, red sandstone jail that sits near a creek that flows into the Brazos River. Dr. T. Lindsay Baker gives a good history of the town in his book, *Ghost Towns of Texas.*

He told how the town was named after Claire Becker, daughter of R.L. Rhomberg, an early rancher and settler in the area. The town once had several newspapers and businesses, but, because of the lack of an adequate water supply, falling cotton prices, and the moving of local oil camps, it went into a decline that brought about the county seat being moved to Jayton in the 1950s. Shortly after records were transferred to the new county seat, the old courthouse burned. Then the post office closed in the 1970s.

"The only resident that I know of in Clairemont is the man who delivers mail in this area," a rancher who lives near Jayton told me. On the day we visited the town site, even this man was not at home. We stopped at the old jail. Somebody had painted red hearts on its walls along with other graffiti. I walked inside and was amazed at the thick walls of native sandstone that had been hacked from the local countryside. I remembered coming here one day in August when the temperature had been near 100 degrees. Yet when I walked inside the old jail, the temperature must have dropped fifteen degrees because of the natural insulation provided by its thick walls.

Nearby is another sandstone building with sagging windows and frames hammered and stripped by time. A sign reads, "Welcome to Clairemont. Gone but not forgotten." Near it is an empty business with most of the windows broken. I walked inside and the stale smell of vacancy and age greeted me. Pieces of insulation hung from broken ceiling beams like torn intestines from an animal hit by a semi. I walked outside and looked at the deserted streets. Patches of clouds floated overhead, making beautiful white dots in the brilliantly blue sky. I looked at the car. Eddie and Norm had already returned to the vehicle, had it started, and were ready to leave. Obviously they were not as turned on by the visit as I was. We had originally planned to camp near the old jail. But, because the many empty beer cans around indicated to us that the site probably was used extensively for nightly beer drinking sessions, we decided to stay at a motel. So we drove to Rotan and checked in at the Wind Word Inn, a small but clean facility.

After dinner everybody went back to their rooms. I poured myself a drink and walked outside. I looked at the clouds blotting out the moon. I sensed the night odors coming in with the darkness. I leaned back against the wall. I wished we had taken our chances at the old jail.

Chapter Eighteen

We heard many wild stories
About broncs and bad dogs
And, in the Panhandle, they said
Watch out for those wild hogs.
Walk across Texas
With its wonderful sights.
Walk across Texas
With its beautiful nights.

I joined the ranks of the blister boys on this day. After showering I discovered a blister on my fourth toe. Norm and Eddie had already suffered blisters so I figured I was in good company. I remembered two days ago when Norm had discovered a blister and Eddie had given him a piece of sandpaper to sand down the skin left after the blister had been drained. Norm said it had not hurt. So I walked to Eddie's room and asked him to check my toe. His athletic trainer background again came in handy this day and many other times on the trip.

"Let's look at that toe," he said. He put on his glasses and looked like one of those old time doctors pictured in a Norman Rockwell painting. "Yeah, you got a blister but it's not a big one and it doesn't look red. Let me drain it and put some ointment and tape on it and I think you'll be all right."

I gave him one of my disposable syringes that I use for my insulin injections. He drained the blister, added the ointment and tape, and pronounced me ready for the road.

"Are you sure I shouldn't just quit this whole thing?" I asked in jest.

He shook his head. "You remember what you said your buddy, Doug, told you when things got a little tough, don't you? When the going gets tough, the tough get going."

I pulled on two pair of wool socks over the taped toe. It felt fine. I said, "Well, let's try it."

The weather was perfect for walking. The temperature stood in the lower fifties with a stiff wind from the north that meant we would be getting a push from it. We started about fifteen miles south of Spur and headed for Rotan. I looked at the raw, red-colored draws on the side of the road. They were lined with mesquite and junipers and a flower that looked like a sunflower with a burst of yellow at its top. I stopped and found a rock to sit on. I pulled off my shoe and sock and looked at my foot. It looked and felt okay. I kept walking.

A large pickup truck with a trailer pulled over when it met me. The driver rolled down the window and offered his hand in a fierce handshake. "Howdy," he said. "I'm Joe Nixon. Are you one of them fellers (that word is used for fellows out here in West Texas. Nobody called us fellows, it was always fellers.) walking across Texas?"

As I shook his hand, I told him that we were the men walking across Texas. He had strong fingers that looked like he could drive a nail into a fence post with them if he chose to.

"Daggone it, I had hoped we could have made contact earlier. We were gonna invite you boys to come out to the ranch and stay."

We talked about his life and how he wound up in West Texas. He said that his wife attended college in Tyler and got her nursing degree. Then they decided to move out here. "I love this country. Nobody knows your business but you," he said. "I normally don't get on this side of the fence. I like to stay on the other side where I live. No bad news over there. I get on this side, and I'm like an ostrich with his head stuck in the sand."

We talked about West Texas and I told him I had been reared there. We both knew an old-time cattleman named Buster Welch. He had sold cattle to my father, who had once owned the cattle auction at Midland. I had even worked cattle a couple of times with Buster Welch. Then Nixon talked about some of the wild animals that lived in the area.

"I saw a badger this morning," he said. "A big 'un. He was running on the other side of that fence."

He started his pickup. "Why don't you boys think it over and come on back and spend the night. If you decide to, just come to that gate behind me and go on in. Drive about a mile down that road and you'll come to our house. If there's not anybody there, just go on in and get on the radio and say, 'We're here,' and somebody will come on up out of the pasture and greet you."

He left and I kept walking. I stopped for a drink and looked to the northwest where Duck Creek cut through the country. It got its name because of the flocks of ducks that swam on its water holes and small lakes. I reached the car and then drove and picked up Eddie and Norm. We passed a sign that said, "Buying live wild hogs." We stopped for a look. A corral made of steel panels stood behind a loading chute. Several hogs looked at us. They had a variety of colors ranging from reds to blacks and whites. They squealed as we approached the pen.

"Boys, I think they are wild hogs," said Eddie. "They're mean looking anyway."

We drove into Rotan and stopped at *The Roby Star Record/Rotan Advance* newspaper, owned and published by Rosemary Donham. She was instantly friendly. She said she graduated from high school here, got

Wild hogs run plentiful in the Texas Panhandle and are bought for meat at hog buying stations like this one located north of Jayton. Photos by Eddie Lane and Norm Snyder.

married, and then they moved to Fort Worth. Her husband worked for General Dynamics.

"But, he was an old country boy and I tell you, you can take the boy out of the country, but you can't take the country out of the boy. So we moved back here."

She said she bought the newspaper in 1998. Her prior experience included working for the owner. "He had an old Olivetti typewriter that he wrote his stories on. He just beat that thing to death," she said. "When I went to work for him, I was a story gatherer and I also sold advertising. I learned it all."

I asked her if she missed living in the big city of Fort Worth. She shook her head. "Not at all. Out here, the people are the most wonderful people in the world. They are a community with a heart and they will do anything for you."

Eddie came into the office and introduced himself. He said he had gotten gasoline at a local station and the man not only insisted on filling the car, but also washed the windshields. "Talk about full service," he said. She nodded her head and said the station's owner was Dwight Lee and that kind of thing was why she liked living here. Eddie told about buying a photograph of Sammy Baugh, the famed football player from this area who played for the Washington Redskins during the 1940s.

"Let me tell you a story about Sammy Baugh," she said. "A man I know had a bull out and he was trying to get him back inside his fence. This feller stopped his truck and got out and helped him get that bull back in the pasture. The man thanked him and told the man that he seemed to know a lot about cattle. The man said, 'I should. I have been ranching for years in this country. My name is Sammy Baugh.'" Then he got in his truck and left. That man just stood there, having a hard time figuring why somebody as famous as Sammy Baugh had stopped and helped him get a bull back into his pasture."

We ate lunch at a place called Tater and Toads and then drove back to the wild hog buying station. I definitely wanted to meet the person who ran this operation. I'm not sure what I expected this person to look like. But, that image certainly did not match Sherri Murdock, who greeted us as she unloaded a trailer full of wild hogs. She's thirty-eight, lanky, and has an appealing outdoor attractiveness about her. She also has a degree in cardio-vascular critical nursing care from the University of Iowa. Certainly, not the kind of person you'd expect to be weighing wild hogs and buying them by the pound.

"My brother has three stations where he buys the wild hogs," she said. "He moved to Big Spring so I took over this station. Most of the hogs that we buy are domestic hogs that have gotten out and become wild hogs. After we buy them, we ship them to San Antonio where they are slaughtered. Then we ship the meat to Europe where it is considered a delicacy."

Larry Callan, who had backed his trailer loaded with wild hogs up to the unloading chute, watched as the hogs got ready to run off the trailer and into the waiting pens. "They're good eating," he said. "But, if they've been eating this schinery brush, they might not taste as good as others. And, another thing, you sure don't want to run over one. They are like hitting a piece of concrete. Once I hit one and thought he weighed 300 pounds. I was wrong. He only weighed ninety-one pounds."

He said he traps the hogs on his ranch. He uses bait made from corn syrup, peanut butter, dog food, and table scraps. Then he spreads corn all over the ground around the traps. "That brings them in pretty good," he said.

Murdock said she pays from fifteen cents to fifty cents per pound for the hogs. The ones that weigh the most bring the most per pound. "A boar that weighs 250 or more will bring fifty cents a pound," she said. "And, anyone who brings in a hog that weighs more than 101 pounds gets a five dollar per head bonus."

Callan watched as Murdock tallied the weight of the hogs he had unloaded. "They tear up your fences and pasture," he said. "That's why we try to get rid of them." Murdock said the hogs also dig up yards around homes. So will they attack a human? "No," she said. "If you got one hemmed up in a corner, he might run at you. But, most of them will run away from a person."

Callan said he likes to load the hogs at night when they can't see you. "It's a lot easier," he said. "Load them at night, and all they can do is smell you and that doesn't cause them to act too crazy when you run them into the trailer."

Murdock said she had a friend named Barefoot Bob Richardson. "He knows more about wild hogs than anybody around here," she said. "The *New York Times* did an article on the hogs not too long ago and they quoted Barefoot Bob in their article. I've been out with him several times when he goes out and runs his traps. He does know a lot about hogs."

We watched her make the tally on her scales and then pay Callan in cash. He thanked her and drove away. We shook her hand and wished her the best of luck. "If you ever want to take advantage of that nursing degree, give me a call," said Eddie. "I've got a daughter who works in the cardiac infant critical care unit at Harris Hospital in Fort Worth."

She smiled. "I might do that. But, you know, I kinda like this job. It's out in the country and you are your own boss and well, it's different and I enjoy it," she said.

We drove back to our motel. I called the Nixons and asked if we could come for dinner instead of spending the night. I talked to Sherri Nixon and explained that we had already set our computers and gear up in the motel. She said she would be glad to fix our supper.

I decided to give my foot a rest for the afternoon and stay at the motel and work on my notes. Norm and Eddie drove to where we had stopped walking to continue our march to Roby. En route, Eddie met another walker named Paul Hanson. "I've walked the Clear Fork of the Brazos, I don't know how many times. I know it as well as I do the floor of my kitchen," he said. "I've found hundreds of arrow heads." He showed Eddie some of the arrowheads he had found on a recent walk and told him to be careful on the rest of his walk.

Meanwhile, back at the motel, the wind became very strong. I listened to it howling outside my room and thought of my days as a youngster in West Texas and how lonely that wind sounded out there when I had been by myself waiting for my older brother or my parents to come home. Listen to the wind long enough and it will do things to your emotions, making you think of things you shouldn't be thinking of and imagining all kinds of monsters and bad hombres hovering outside waiting to come in and plunge a knife or dagger into your stomach. I was glad when Eddie and Norm returned and we got ready to visit the Nixons.

By the time we arrived at their house, the temperature had dropped to near forty degrees. Joe and Sherri greeted us and introduced us to their sons, Trayven, fifteen, and Daylon, thirteen. Joe told us that the boys wanted to take us for a ride over the 27,000-acre ranch on which he managed the cattle. So we climbed into a pickup and Tray, carrying a .22 caliber rifle, got behind the wheel and began our tour. Both youngsters were friendly and talkative.

"We have two buffalo, bunches of quail, coyotes, badgers, rattlesnakes, cattle, and hogs on this place," said Tray. "Matter of fact, we say that everything out here will either stick you, sting you, or bite you."

He pointed at some grass growing near clumps of gramma grass and Spanish Daggers and mesquites. "That is called eyebrow grass," he said. "If you look at it, it looks just like an eyebrow." We looked and he was right. It did look like an eyebrow on one of the old character actors in the early day movies. Tray stopped the truck and pointed to a spot beyond some brush. "There's a buck standing there," he said. I looked and looked and finally I saw the animal looking back at us. He twitched his white tail.

"We've also got rattlesnakes galore in here," he said. "The record for the ranch is a snake that had seventeen rattlers and a button." We continued our drive and I asked if they liked to eat wild hog. "Oh, yeah," said Tray. "We practically live off the meat from the piglets. They are really tender."

They both go to school in Jayton and Daylon plays on the high school six-man football team. The mascot is the Jaybirds. "I play both defense and offense," he said. "Of course we only got eight boys on our whole team." Tray stopped the truck at the top of a steep incline that appeared to be extremely muddy. "We'd better check this out," he said. Both boys got out and walked to the bottom of the incline. They shook their heads and came back. "We'd better not try that today. It is pretty darn muddy and it's a long way to the house if we got stuck," said Tray. We headed back for the house. Tray stopped at some huge holes along the road. "Those are badger holes," he said.

We kept driving. I asked if the boys liked this country better than East Texas that has so many pines and other trees, the area where they had spent their childhood. They studied the question a moment and then the older one responded. "I sorter miss the trees," he said. "But, this ranch, well, it is awesome. Like where we live is the tallest point in this part of the country. You can get out at night and see the lights of Rotan and if you look really hard you can see the red lights on that windmill farm which is just outside of Snyder. And, the sunsets. You have never seen anything like the sunsets out here."

We arrived back at the house. Tray parked the truck. We climbed out and saw we were in time to experience one of the sunsets. There were layers of red twisted around some dark blue clouds. Other orange colored ribbons had sneaked into the setting. It was indeed awesome.

We went inside to eat. Sherri had prepared chicken fried steak and all of the trimmings. She stopped me and said, "I read about your having diabetes and know you probably have to watch what you eat. So I made you some steak without all of the batter. And, I cooked some of the vegetables in water so you won't have to worry about butter being in them," she said. I felt a warmness inside and my words kind of ran together as I thanked her. The food was delicious.

We ate and talked and then said we had to go back to town. The senior Nixon bid goodbye with a strong handshake and an invitation to come back and stay with them whenever we were in this area. Tray and Daylon said they would lead us to the gate at the highway. Tray walked to the pickup carrying his .22 rifle. I asked him, "Do you sleep with that?" He smiled, "Yeah, I certainly do. You don't ever know when you might need it."

We followed them to the ranch entrance. They stopped and opened the massive steel gate. As we started to drive through, we stopped. I asked them what they wanted to be when they left home. Both answered without hesitation. "I want to be a taxidermist," said Dayton. His brother listened and then said, "I want to study wild life management and maybe become a game warden. I think I would like that."

We shook their hands and started driving back to the town. The big slice of the moon that sent showers of light down at us looked beautiful.

Chapter Nineteen

We kept thinking about the Nixons
Who had invited us to dinner
We met their two sons
And, Sherri's cooking was a winner.
Walk across Texas
With its wonderful sights.
Walk across Texas
With its beautiful nights.

When Norm read an advertisement about an alpaca ranch in the area through which we would be walking on this day, he said he would really like to see it. "Alpacas have always fascinated me," he said.

I said that anyone who raises alpacas in this part of the country would be worth talking to. So at the end of our walk, we headed down a two-lane road seeking the AU Golden Alpaca Ranch outside of Hamlin. After about thirty minutes of searching, we finally found the ranch, owned by Alan and Marian Tripp. She seemed surprised we had stopped. "We've been in the business for four years. We have twelve alpacas. We actually breed them and raise the crias (baby alpaca). When a mother is due to give birth, we say we are on the cria watch."

She led us to the corrals where the alpacas were eating alfalfa hay. The animals made a humming noise and were quite friendly. They also spit. One that I was petting looked at my notebook and spit on it. Aw, well, not everybody is impressed with a big-time, hotshot writer and long distance walker. Marian laughed at the incident and told how they shear the animals once a year. They each produce about eight pounds of wool. The alpacas are not cheap.

"No, a breeding female starts at about $10,000," said Marian. "Ours were more expensive than that." So how in the world did they get into raising alpacas? "We were retired and living in Arizona. We saw a story on television about them and decided we would try raising them."

So how did they wind up in a part of West Texas that is known for its cattle and horses and certainly not alpacas? "We found this place on the Internet. And, no we had never been here or knew anything about the country," she said.

She said the alpaca fleece makes wonderful vests, sweaters, and hats. She makes the vests and hats. "A vest sells for $75," she said. "They will last forever. I have a pair of socks that is five years old and they are still like new." A sign hanging inside the barn told about the alpaca fleece. "Alpacas are prized for their luxurious and costly fiber that is harvested once a year. An alpaca sweater or blanket is a cherished possession, frequently handed down from generation to generation. Alpacas are a herd animal that are native to the Andes Mountains of South America. They are very gentle and make wonderful pets."

We wished her the best in her venture and headed for our motel in Rotan. But, after driving about two miles, we discovered a ghost town called Neinda. An old building that once housed Brown's General Merchandise sat on what apparently had been the main street. A Coca-Cola sign hung precariously from the old front porch that was falling down. Time had reduced several other buildings to just piles of lumber. Down the street sat the Neinda Baptist Church, which according to a historical marker had been organized July 21, 1889. We walked inside the gaunt, fading white-painted structure. The stale smell of age lay heavy in the auditorium. Outside, I could hear crows going, "Caw. Caw. Caw. Caw." I looked out of the smoky glass in the windows. Eddie and Norm had already gone back to the car. I lingered a few more minutes and thought of the old-time gospel songs that had been sung in this building, ringing loudly during summertime meetings. I finally walked outside and joined my companions.

Earlier that day a north wind and a temperature in the lower forties had greeted us as we began walking. We all had checked our blisters and Eddie said they looked okay. We stopped at the Roby courthouse for a short look at the modern, plain structure. A historical marker said that Robert E. Lee, who later became the general of the south's Confederate troops, served in this country during the army's punitive measures against the Indians.

I remembered another point of history about this county, named for Samuel Rhoads Fisher. He was a signer of the Texas Declaration of Independence. A bitter struggle erupted in 1886 when the county was organized. Both Roby and Fisher wanted the county seat to be located in their city. An election was held, and Roby won. But, many people questioned the vote and claimed a fraud had been committed after it was discovered that someone named Bill Pup had voted. Mister Pup turned out to be a dog whose owner lived near Roby.

We drove around the town square and looked at some empty buildings and the boarded up Roby Theater. A poster advertised the movie *Shane*, which apparently had been one of the last movies shown there. It was here that we turned off Highway 70 and started our walk on Highway 180 that would lead us on the last part of our journey.

I started my section of the walk beside a cotton field that had been plowed and planted with winter grain. I passed a set of working corrals and could immediately tell a difference in the highways. There was much more traffic on Highway 180. The wind had died a little so the walking was pleasant. I walked through mesquite flats on both sides of the roadway. A form of bluestem grass with waving heads grew abundantly in the pastures. The grass heads looked like silver sheets hanging barely off the ground.

Far off I could hear a ranch dog barking, going, "Oooofa. OOOOfa. Oooofa." Then some cattle joined in with their "mooa, moooa, moooa" cries. What a joy such an early morning concert is.

I came to a bridge. My blister had started hurting so I stopped and pulled off my shoe for a check. I removed the tape and the skin looked all right so I put it back on and continued. The cries of a flock of wild geese heading south echoed from the sky. I looked up and spotted them and thought, "God, what a sight they are." I don't know why, but I waved at them.

I walked across the Clear Fork of the Brazos. It had enough water to flow. Shortly after I crossed the bridge I came to the car, got in, and drove down the highway to pick up Eddie. He said he had had a good walk and told about a black Labrador dog charging out of a farmhouse. "He didn't know whether to attack me or be friendly," said Eddie. "He finally began wagging his tail and watched me walk on down the road like he was telling me 'Bye, bye, Buddy. And, be careful.'"

We stopped at a marker for Woods Chapel Cemetery. We read that a small frame building near this site was used as a church and school. Among the first settlers to the area was Henry Clay Lyon, who is buried in the cemetery. However, his family was buried in the Roby Cemetery. During the Texas Centennial in 1936, plans to rebury him at Roby next to his wife were never completed. The remains of what looked like an old service station with leaning, creaking wooden frames stood nearby.

We drove into Anson and stopped at the Chamber of Commerce office. Angela Ramirez, manager, said the town was getting ready for a Friday night football game and it was so important that it was going to be televised. She was also getting ready for the annual Fall Mesquite Daze. "We'll have vendors set up all around the square," she said. She told us she graduated from high school here and then left for seventeen years when she lived in McAllen and published a real estate magazine for twelve years. "But, my parents live here and my son wanted to be close to them, so we came back," she said.

We walked next door to chat with Jessica Elkens, owner and publisher of *The Western Observer*, the local newspaper. The newspaper is in the front part of the building and a clothing store is in the back. "I'm twenty-four and yes, I enjoy living here," she said. "The people are very supportive and care about you. Like when my son was born, he only weighed three pounds, nine ounces, but everybody rallied around me and it was just wonderful how everybody cares. He's doing fine now."

We left her office and decided to take the side trip to Hamlin that is north on Highway 83. It is a quiet little country town. As we drove through the streets, we saw a long line of fence posts. Stuck on top of each one was a teakettle. We stopped and I knocked on the door. Linda Hill greeted me and laughed about the teakettles. "I have people from all over stopping and asking about those," she said. "I first built the fence. Those are homemade cement blocks and came from a building in Peacock that was torn down in 1917 by a tornado. A woman gave them to my husband and me. We are painters and roofers and were doing a job for her. The fence just kinda happened after that. We stacked them up and then my son got the posts and we stuck them into the concrete blocks. Then I began putting the teakettles on top of the posts. I have bought a few of them and people have donated others." She also has an array of other articles that she has painted in bright colors.

These include some yellow painted discs that came from an old plow. And, just beyond them are old round rubber tractor tires that are also painted different colors. "I wanted the discs to look like sunflowers," she said. So I asked if she had any trouble with people stealing the objects. She laughed. "I don't know why anyone would steal any of this . . . like the teakettles, they're just old teakettles. Why would anyone steal one of those?"

Jon McConal puts on his shoes at the trio's camping site near Perryton. They called the tent trailer in the background, for which Eddie Lane paid $300, the Highway Hilton. Photos by Eddie Lane and Norm Snyder.

Later that night as I pulled off my shoes and looked at my blister, I thought I could change some of her words and pretty much summarize my feeling by asking, "Why would anyone walk 450 miles?" I rubbed the toe with the blister. I smiled and answered my own question by saying out loud, "To see people like the woman with the teakettles on her fence posts." I wondered what tomorrow would bring as I lay down and went to sleep.

Chapter Twenty

When we passed mile 250
Eddie proclaimed
"We're halfway home
In this crazy game."
Walk across Texas
With its wonderful sights.
Walk across Texas
With its beautiful nights.

Eddie made an announcement this morning that lifted our spirits. By continuing our present pace, we should be in Granbury on October 31. I could not believe that we were this close to home and our great adventure was actually nearly two-thirds complete.

We drove to where we had ended walking yesterday. We began walking east toward Anson. Eddie passed a place called the Saddle Shack, owned and operated by Jan Burns. When he told her about our walk, she said he would be interested in her mother who was born in Yosemite National Park and had lived in a tent for the first four years of her life.

As I walked through the country with its tall grasses and loads of mesquite trees, I remembered a bit of history I had read about the vast buffalo herds that once roamed this area. The buffalo hunters lived off the buffalo for several years before killing the last animal in 1879. They left and were followed by people called the bone haulers who found where massive kills had been made. They hauled the bones that remained to market where they were ground and used for bone meal and other items.

A rancher pulled his pickup over and asked if I needed some help. I told him, "No. We're on a 450-mile walk across Texas." His son looked out the window and said, "Man, that's awesome." The father shook his head and said, "Yeah. Well, everybody's got to be doing something."

I continued walking until I rejoined Eddie and Norm. Norm said he had made an interesting discovery beneath a bridge east of Anson. So we drove there for a look. We stopped at the bridge and climbed down a steep embankment. Norm pointed at two abandoned grocery carts. A pile of bones that might have been the remainder of a cooked chicken lay nearby.

We walked under the bridge, which had hundreds of mud nests made by swallows. We found another cart with a bunch of grass resembling a bed piled near it. Beside that were several cigarette butts and a cigar. "This might have been somebody's temporary home," said Eddie.

We left and drove to Anson, the seat of Jones County, once known as Jones City. It was named after Anson Jones, the last president of the Republic of Texas. In a brochure listing all of the many reasons to move to Anson, the old restored Anson Opera House is listed along with a statement that says, "Life is too short not to live in Anson, the crossroads of West Texas."

North of Anson is Stamford, a town that once had a police chief named George G. Flournoy. He kept order largely through his reputation reinforced by a daily routine of target shooting at a stump outside of city hall. He had splintered the stump with the repeated hits from his revolver. Another historical site in the county is Fort Phantom Hill, one of several forts built across the Texas frontier in the early 1850s to protect the westward moving settlers. A letter written by a visitor to the site in 1892 said the fort contained nothing but "one hotel, one saloon, one general store, one blacksmith shop, and 10,000 prairie dogs."

After Anson, we soon crossed the Clear Fork of the Brazos, running full with fast-moving chocolate-colored water. Shortly after that we moved into Shackelford County and came to some well-built cattle-working pens owned by the Chimney Creek Ranch. We stopped and looked at the pens that had a solid looking loading chute made of steel and thick lumber. A giant hand crank is used to raise and lower the loading platform. A sign read, "Bud Matthews, Texas." Massive mesquites grew along the corral fence and a marker read, "The trail of the Butterfield Overland Mail passed this point in 1858."

The site had a red railroad cattle car parked nearby. Somebody had stolen a marker from the car sitting on a piece of a track. Nearby, another sign read, "Texas Central—Bud Matthews Switch 1900–1967. Chimney Creek Ranch, Shackelford County, Texas."

Far off to the south were the wavering lines of some of those giant windmills that produce electricity.

In the northwest corner of Shackelford county lies a strip of sand that is one mile wide and twenty-five miles long, making a scar in the county that was originally open prairie but now consists of liberal growths of mesquite and chaparral. Cottonwood, mulberry, pecan elm, hackberry, and willow trees line the creek banks.

We drove into Albany and saw a giant sign welcoming people and proclaiming the city to be "Home of the Hereford." The city was named for Albany, Georgia, and cattle drivers going up the Western Trail to Dodge City used the town as a supply point. Discovery of the Cook oilfield in 1926 and later discoveries have fostered the development of Albany into an oil drilling, producing, and supply center.

We asked directions to the Old Jail Art Center. It is housed inside a restored 1878 limestone building that was the first permanent jail in the county seat. Inside this center is an unbelievable art collection including collections of Chinese tomb figures dating from the third century b.c., pre-Columbian art, and nineteenth and twentieth century paintings and sculptures from such masters as Henry Moore, Pablo Picasso, Amedeo Modigliani, Giacomo Manzu, and John Marin.

Holly Phillips, a tall attractive woman with long black hair who is an administrative assistant at the center, welcomed us. She moved to Albany two years ago from Fort Worth and said she found the city and county to be an exciting place to live. "We have quality things here to do and see," she said. She introduced us to Margaret Blagg, executive director of the center. She eyed us and our walking outfits with skepticism at first, but finally seemed to accept the fact that we were not just vagabonds looking for handouts.

"A lot of towns have an old building but they don't have anything to put inside it," she said. "We were blessed with both." But, it took the efforts of local resident Robert Nail. When he learned that the old jail that had been vacant for years might be demolished, he bought the structure and the land. He repaired the building's roof and widows and created an office and studio inside. Nail died in 1968 and again the old jail became vacant until 1980 when the art center was created.

As Blagg related this history, she led us by old steel cell doors with leg irons and chains still hanging from the walls. We walked upstairs and stood among selections from Bill Bomar's collection of some 280 crosses from around the world. Bomar, an artist, was reared in Fort Worth and his family had strong ties to Albany. We looked at a pastel on paper done by Emily Guthrie Smith, entitled *Summer Sledding*. The work captures children sliding down a hill on pieces of cardboard.

I asked her how and why such a collection of fine art would find a home in this part of West Texas that is more known for its high school football teams and sprawling cattle ranches. "From the earliest times, some of the ranchers in this area sent their children away to schools like Princeton. As a matter of fact, at one time, we had more Princeton graduates per capita than any other place in the nation," she said. "But, these people are well educated and well traveled and have an appreciation for the finer things." She also credits an annual event called the Fandangle with creating an opportunity for local youngsters to perform. Nail, who was Princeton-educated, created the Fandangle, an outdoor musical that tells the story of early settlers and the conflicts they faced through music, dance and narration. He wrote the musical after creating the office in the old jail.

We thanked her for her time and the tour and left for a visit to the Presbyterian and Episcopal church buildings. We first went to the Presbyterian church. The smell of old song books and velvet cushions greeted us as we sat and looked at the beautiful stained glass windows, which made showers of vibrant colors as the sun hit them. We also looked at the church's famous pipe organ with silver-looking pipes sticking from the dark colored wood cabinet. Sitting there, I recalled a time in my younger days when I was working in Colorado and three friends and I had gone to Idaho Springs for two days. We had no money and had found ourselves on deserted streets late at night as the mountain cold moved into the city. We found a Catholic church just as a biting rain with chunks of ice began falling. We lay down on the back seats, seeking warmth and sleep. We found both and stayed there for four hours before a priest found us, accused us of being hippies, and ushered us out into the cold. Those were the days.

Nobody gave us such a greeting here. We left and went to the Episcopal church where Hazel Hopkins saw us and led us inside the building built in 1889, the oldest church structure in Albany. William Aikman in London made the stained glass windows for a church near York, England. George Jardine & Son of New York City made the organ in 1859 for St. John's Episcopal Church in Oneida, N.Y. The organ's case is made from gothic revival chestnut and has gilded facade pipes. The organ was restored in 1991 and given to Trinity Episcopal Church by Ted Blankenship.

"I was not raised Episcopalian," said Hopkins. "Oh, my goodness no. I was raised a Baptist. But, I had a son who had asthma and we moved here and this church was the closest one to us. So we began coming here and the people were so nice that we became Episcopalians. And, you are welcome here anytime."

We thanked her and drove back to our motel. We went inside Eddie's room for a drink. We talked about how full our day had been and about the art and people in Albany. We pulled off our shoes and checked our blisters. They were okay. We had another drink and then ate dinner at a local steak house. We came back and I sat in my room alone. I could hear the public address system from the local high school football stadium. Somebody had told us Albany was playing Winters in a crucial game. I could hear the drum going, "Boom. Boom. Boom."

I listened and smiled and thought, "Well, it's Friday night and we're in Texas and football still makes as loud an echo in people's lives around here as do the Picassos and Manzus in the Old Jail Art Center." I slept soundly.

Chapter Twenty-one

We came into Albany
A town that's been blest
With lots of things
From the old west.
Walk across Texas
With its wonderful sights.
Walk across Texas
With its beautiful nights.

This rugged country of Shackelford County has been home to some equally rugged characters from the past. One of those was John Selman, a gunman who shot and killed several people while he served as a lawman.

Selman moved to Fort Griffin in the 1870s where he became a deputy for Shackelford County's sheriff John M. Larn. There was little the two did not do in terrorizing the county. However, after a vigilante group locked Larn in jail and shot him to death, Selman moved to Lincoln County, New Mexico where he organized a group of thugs known as Selman's Scouts. They were accused of murder, rape, and robbery.

Selman eventually moved to El Paso where he made his living gambling and serving as a constable. He killed a former Texas Ranger during a brawl at a brothel. He also shot and killed the famous gunman John Welsey Hardin during a dice game. But, he lost a fight with U.S. Deputy Marshal George Scarborough, when Scarborough shot Selman four times. The bad man died during surgery on April 6, 1890.

I told Eddie and Norm about Selman as we drove to our walking point about eight miles east of Albany. The weather was perfect and the wind was at our backs as we began. Also, all our blisters appeared to be healed. I thought of some of the reactions we had received when people first greeted us. When looking at Eddie and myself I could understand the reactions. Eddie wore shorts that had been patched with duct tape and carried a walking stick made from PVC pipe. I had on shorts that were too large and my T-shirt spilled from the back of them, hanging down past the leg end of the shorts. And, Norm, well, actually, you could consider him the best dressed of the group.

We ate lunch at a roadside park and continued walking and came to a huge set of sculptured antlers sitting in a pasture with the grass mown around them. They stood about eight feet tall and looked like they were made from steel. The skull looked like it was made from fiberglass. But, that

The three walkers discovered several unusual art objects during their walk. One was this massive set of steel antlers between Breckenridge and Palo Pinto. There was no information at the scene to indicate who had made them. Photos by Eddie Lane and Norm Snyder.

is just a guess because there is nothing to explain who made the antlers or why they are there. A nearby sign gives the name of a ranch but it also has a posted and private property sign. They do attract attention as several other cars stopped while we were there.

Two miles past the antlers, I stopped to look at the remains of an old oil well drilling rig that had been pulled to a pasture and left. It's a mass of huge wooden beams, bolts, and cables. A piece of it sat in some small mesquite trees and Spanish dagger grass. I wondered if its owner had ever struck oil and thought of the stories of success or failure it could tell. Clots of yellow broom weed grew between the boards and steel on the old tower.

I reached the car and drove to pick up Norm and Eddie. We stopped on the edge of Albany to look at a park that had some old oil field equipment on display. I read a historical marker that said this was the site of the Cook Ranch Oil Field. It told about William Ivy Cook and his wife, Matilda, buying 27.75 sections of ranching country here in 1895. During the early booms, Cook sold mineral leases but said he could drink from his hat all of the oil under his land. But, after his death, Matilda leased all of the acreage and drillers struck oil at 1,241 feet on their second attempt. That well flowed at 1,000 barrels a day. Since then, the ranch has produced 825 wells. Mrs. Cook used part of that money to found the W.I. Cook Memorial Hospital in Fort Worth in 1929.

We had discovered the Weaver-Oates Pharmacy and returned for a visit. Norm found a seat outside and began removing the tiny cactus spines that stuck into his fingers while he was picking prickly pear cactus fruit. "The fruit was juicy but filled with seeds," he said. "They looked like a pomegranate with lots of red juice."

Eddie and I walked inside the pharmacy that has the old style soda fountain. I ordered a diet Dr Pepper and looked at the tile floors and steel tile ceilings. I walked around and saw a sign advertising Pangburn Chocolates and English Leather Toiletries for men. I stopped at a candy cabinet that had Snickers, Butterfingers, and Baby Ruths. Beside it was a nice display of pocketknives that included Case and Puma brands. I went to the drug counter and introduced myself to Howard Todd, owner and pharmacist. He said he once threw the *Star-Telegram* on a paper route.

"I bought this in 1977," he said. "It is full of history. Look what I found under a pile of pipe in the back."

He showed bottles used for prescriptions in the early days of the store. One still had the label on it that read, "Lloyd's Hydrastis and Potichlor." He smiled as he thought about those days. "I may know more than they did," he said. "But, they actually did more work than I did. Because if they filled twenty prescriptions, it probably meant they had to make mixtures from five or six ingredients for each one." He showed one prescription that called for six ingredients for a stomach ailment. "Nowadays, we spend all of our time looking at the computer," he said. "Back then, they spent their time looking at and mixing the drugs."

We looked some more and then we left. Norm had gotten most of the stickers out of his fingers. We decided to drive around and look at the country.

As we drove through the mesquite-covered hills east of the city, I remembered reading about a meteorite that had been found there called the "Texas Iron." The Caddo Indians, who had a sky-oriented religion, called the rock the Medicine Rock. It weighed 1,635 pounds, and for years many thought the gigantic stone was a platinum nugget. The rock is now in the Peabody Museum of Natural History at Yale where it is known as "Red River."

We also passed close to the site where the Ledbetter Salt Works once stood. William Henry Ledbetter founded the salt works on a spring described by early settlers as gushing water that was "salty as brine but bitter and muddy." Ledbetter learned how to put the water into barrels and let it settle. Then he would boil the remains in pots until only the salt remained. Salt was like gold in those days since it was needed to cure meat and to feed livestock. The salt was stored in burlap bags and hauled to Weatherford for sale. Ledbetter abandoned the salt works in 1880 due to a lack of rail transportation.

We returned to our motel in Albany. After dinner I sat in my room. I looked at a sign that read, "Hunters, please use the provided game shed for cleaning game. Please be courteous enough to leave the shed area clean. Bird feathers, intestines, etc. are to be placed inside the plastic bag. Then in the dumpster. A cleaning fee will be charged to you if game is cleaned in the room."

I guessed the sign was necessary, though it was unusual. An employee told me that it was not unusual to find deer carcasses hanging inside the bathroom where they had been cleaned. However, I must admit the room was spacious and clean during my visit. I poured myself a drink and thought, "This is not a whole lot different than the good old days."

Chapter Twenty-two

We remembered crossing the Red River
With water that looked like blood
Oldtimers had told us
The Red often went on a flood.
Walk across Texas
With its wonderful sights.
Walk across Texas
With its beautiful nights.

Norm and I decided to go to church this morning. Eddie said he would start walking to Breckenridge that lay some twenty-four miles to the east and we could join him after church. "I don't think I will be in Breckenridge by then," he said. He laughed.

So we drove to Trinity Episcopal Church that had its first recorded service on February 25, 1878, when an evening prayer was held in the then temporary courthouse of Albany. We walked through the lobby that was filled with the smells of coffee and cookies and sat near the back on one of the creaking, wooden seats. The Reverend Rosemary (Roz) Thomas of Abilene delivered the morning prayer and service. She's a slender person with a good strong voice.

I got a good feeling as I sat in the aging, creaking pew. I felt the warmth from the heater that made loud, panting sounds and listened as sounds of coughs and throat clearings echoed in the tiny chapel and Rev. Thomas urged us to be better people. Marc Sanders played the pipe organ. Later, we lingered in the auditorium for a cup of coffee and Rev. Thomas told me that she owned a pickup and a pair of boots so she guessed that qualified her to be a Texan. Two people shook my hand and told me that they had a book inside them but they just hadn't found the time to write the manuscripts.

Sanders told us that he also plays the pipe organ at the Presbyterian church several blocks away. "I'm going to have to hustle to get there," he said. "It takes me about twenty minutes." So he deposited his coffee cup and began a brisk walk to the other church.

We also left and drove east on Highway 180 until we reached Eddie. Then Norm and I started walking from our stations. I walked about two miles and passed a set of corrals made from cedar pickets and railroad cross ties. Four horses stood inside and stared at me when I moved in for a closer look. Suddenly, they began running around the corral, sending explosions of dust from the ground.

I walked back to the highway and noticed that traffic was much heavier than it had been on Highway 70. I walked through some mesquite flats and came to the car. I drove to pick up Eddie and Norm.

We had seen a sign that said Baker's Church lay to the north off the highway. We decided to take a look. We drove down a gravel road for a mile or so and saw nothing. We looked at a large stock tank that had several ducks swimming in it. We stopped and the ducks suddenly took to the air. The sun caught the green on their breasts making a beautiful sight as they soared upward.

We stopped to talk to Jimmy McKay who was feeding his cattle. His son played in some tall grass near their pickup. I asked the father if he were afraid of the son finding a rattlesnake. "Aw, if he keeps stomping in that grass he might and then he'll know better than to play in that stuff," he said. He said he did not know for sure where the old church might be. But he did give us some vague directions and wished us well.

We drove back toward the highway. We passed two deer that were standing with their rumps facing us. We stopped and looked. They bent their heads back toward us for a quick look. Then they continued grazing.

We finally admitted that we were not going to find the church. We stopped and looked at the map. We talked about how far we had walked and how far we lacked.

"I'll tell you something," said Eddie. "We are really not that far away from home. We get to Breckenridge and then there is Palo Pinto, Weatherford, and we're on our last trek. Who would have ever thought that we would make it?"

Norm smiled.

"I did," he said. "I never start anything that I don't fully expect to finish."

I told them that I felt proud of what we had accomplished. "And," I added, "We haven't had a major cuss fight or disagreement."

"That's because we have not discussed religion or politics," said Norm.

We decided to drive on and check the rest of the mileage into Breckenridge. When we arrived there, we ate lunch and drove around the old brick streets. Then we drove back to Albany and the motel. We ate sandwiches and retired for the night.

Chapter Twenty-three

When we walked into Breckenridge
We were feeling the toil
We looked at all those derricks
Many still pumping oil.
Walk across Texas
With its wonderful sights.
Walk across Texas
With its beautiful nights.

We made it a part of our routine to stop at local newspapers and tell them about our walk, and ask about local history and attractions. We also said we would gladly take time out for an interview for a possible story. Everyone we had stopped to talk to seemed appreciative. So after we checked out of our motel, we stopped at the Albany newspaper. The editor barely acknowledged us.

"Uh, aw, I'm sorry but I just don't have the time to talk to you," she said. "I am working on a very big project that will take me to lunch. And, then I've got to go meet somebody for lunch and do a possible interview there. And, then . . ."

I interrupted her. "Well, thanks. We didn't want anything and we are not selling anything. We just thought you might want to interview us and since you obviously do not have the time and are not interested, we'll go on down the road." She looked up briefly and said, "You boys be careful and maybe I'll see you on down the road."

We drove to where we had ended our walk yesterday. Eddie let me out and he and Norm drove to their stations. I began walking and immediately noticed how beautiful the skies were. They looked like somebody had taken a big, blue bowl and stuck it up there. I walked across Hubbard Creek and then came to Hubbard Creek Lake. I realized that I was in Stephens County, which originally was named Buchanan County after President James Buchanan. The county became Stephens County in 1861. The landscape is rugged with hills and has topsoil of red clay on which grow mesquite, hackberry, and elm trees. Broomweed, wild rye, bluestem, and milkweed grow abundantly over the pasturelands.

The early settlers faced a hard life trying to make a living from the country. One schoolteacher said his pen was incapable of doing justice in recording the horrible depredations committed in this territory by the barbaric, uncivilized savages. "But, after the Indians removal, the settlers had to deal with disagreeable peculiarities that included sandstorms in the spring, northers in the winter, traveling grasshoppers in the fall, and long, severe parching droughts in the summer and all other seasons of the year." The droughts were bad. One writer said the drought of 1886–1887 dried up most creeks. "You could follow the bed of the creek by the buzzards that flew over," he wrote.

We drove into Breckenridge, the county seat that originally was called Picketville. The town exploded with growth when oil was struck in 1920. In one year, the Breckenridge oilfield produced fifteen percent of all the oil produced in the United States and supplied one third of the petroleum produced in Texas.

Thousands of workers and speculators came to the county seat and lived in acres of tents and shacks. The boom intensified in 1921 when drillers hit Stoker No. 1 near the edge of the city. Breckenridge quickly became a forest of derricks as more than 200 wells were drilled within the city limits. The oil production was credited with the city's explosive growth that saw the establishment of ten theaters, eighty-nine oil companies, seventy-nine eating places, and two daily newspapers.

We stopped at *The Breckenridge American*, the remaining daily newspaper, and visited with Don Truel, editor. He's a friendly person who looks like Dustin Hoffman or Richard Gere. He laughed at the description and said he preferred the latter.

"I'm from California but please don't tell anybody. I have lived here thirty-one years and I am still trying to get the Texas accent down," he said. "I had never lived in a community smaller than half a million before coming here. But, I love this country and this city."

He worked at a local golf course for several years before becoming sports editor of the newspaper. He talked about the power of high school football. "Football runs this town and always will," he said. "For example, we have won six state titles. Brownwood is the only other town in the area that has more state titles than we do. One year we were headed to state but got beat by Stamford. They called us the best nine and one team in the state."

He urged us to look at the county courthouse, built in the 1920s and called by many as "the best little courthouse in Texas." He also said we should be sure and look at the murals scattered around the city. "The Texas Legislature voted us as the mural capital of Texas in 2001," he said. He gave us a map showing the locations of the murals and we left to look at them.

Billy Ines and Debra Warr painted the murals that depict local scenes captured by Basil Clemons, a photographer who lived in Breckenridge during the 1920s. We looked at one that shows a ranching scene of cattle being branded and another of a street scene during the oil boom. Then we stopped at a mural that has dozens of mirrors sparkling around a sign that reads, "Howdy from Breckenridge. The Dynamo of West Texas." The scene also has a rider on a bucking horse and a well gushing oil. We all thought the murals were good and that the old courthouse was certainly a piece of work.

We drove back to where we had stopped walking, about three miles west of Breckenridge. Eddie and I made the walk. Even though we were close to town, we saw several large herds of cattle. A cowboy riding alone was driving one of the herds toward a set of corrals

Norm waited for us at the city limit sign. We crawled into the car and drove to a motel where we checked in. We had a drink and then ate dinner. We had neglected to ask Don Truel what one does in Breckenridge on a Monday night for entertainment. We retreated to our motel rooms and watched the Dallas Cowboys play the New York Giants. Dallas lost. I missed having Jane there so I could verbalize my displeasure.

Chapter Twenty-four

We stayed at many places
But we'll have to confess
The places where we camped
Were absolutely the best.
Walk across Texas
With its wonderful sights.
Walk across Texas
With its beautiful nights.

Our original plans had been to camp out as much as possible. My back injury had changed that early into the walk and sent us to motels along the way. I figured that I could rest better on a real mattress instead of a pad and air mattress that I used for camping. But within the last few days, my back seemed fine. And, the blisters on our toes had all healed nicely. So we decided to try to find a camping site when we left Breckenridge.

Eddie made a phone call to Mineral Wells State Park, a beautiful camping site where I had stayed many times. The news was not good.

"They are booked up solid through the next three weeks," he said. "So why don't we do a short walk and then drive to Possum Kingdom State Park and see if they have anything."

Norm and I agreed. So we began our walk just east of the Breckenridge city limit signs toward Palo Pinto. After about a mile, I came to pastures that had been burned off in last summer's grass fires that swept through this area. The smell of the fire was still strong. I walked past a black mare that soon would foal. She turned and looked at me. She had a white dot in the center of her forehead that looked like a tiny white star.

I kept walking and passed several herds of Hereford and Angus cattle. They grazed on grass that had not been burned. They looked to be in good shape, their stomachs bulging and full. The brush in the pasture had thickened. I walked past healthy growths of cedar and mesquite. I stopped for a drink of water and sensed the unique smell of a set of working corrals. I looked but could see nothing because of the heavy growth of brush. I told myself, "I'll bet there is a set of corrals in there."

So just for the hell of it, I got off the road and climbed through a fence. I parted the thick limbs of cedars and walked a few more feet. Suddenly, through an opening, there stood the working corrals. The odor of blood from de-hornings and castrations and brandings, along with the smell of cattle, hung strong over the place. I thought back into my earlier days as a youngster when I helped do all of those things. My nose had been right.

I went back to the highway and continued walking. Feather blue stem grew along the bar ditches. It is a tall grass with silver thatches of seeds near the top of the stems. The sun flashed onto those, making them look like silver strings of uncombed hair.

I reached the car. I ate a snack of crackers and drank some juice. I felt homesick. I was ready for this trip to end. I wanted to see Jane and my dog, Cleo, who would lick my hand. I shook my head and drove to pick up Eddie and Norm. After they had loaded themselves, I said, "Let's head to Possum Kingdom Lake." We drove north and west through more ranching country. I remembered something I read about the carbon black industry that came to this area during the oil boom. Carbon black, which is produced from the sour gas from oil wells, was discovered in 1864 by J.K. Wright, a Philadelphia ink maker. But, the process was little used until methods to reduce the high cost of production were perfected, and carbon black became widely used as a reinforcing agent in automobile tires.

Since carbon black comes from the sour gas from oil wells, it was here for the asking when oil was discovered. In 1923, the first carbon black plant was built in Stephens County. Two other plants were built that same year and annual production from the three plants totaled more than two million pounds. By 1926 there were seven carbon black plants in the county and that year Texas produced 20 percent of the nation's carbon black.

We drove over a small creek that had no name posted on the bridge. I knew that we were not too far from a creek with the rather unusual name of Six Shooter Creek. I once tried to find out how it got its name, but nobody seemed to know. When pressed, an old-timer had said, "Hailfire, boy. They used to carry six shooters in those earlier days so I imagine somebody lost their six shooter in this little stream of water and they called it Six Shooter Creek."

We came to the entrance of Possum Kingdom State Park. I had camped here many times and loved it not only for its natural beauty but also for all of the game, including raccoons and deer that wander freely in the camping area. There also are partially furnished cabins. We went inside. They said they were booked and maybe if we came back within a month, we might get a camping site.

We drove out of the state park and headed east. We came to a sign that read, "The world's largest wheelbarrow just ahead." We drove a short distance and there beside the road, painted red with a white frame, was absolutely the largest wheelbarrow I had ever seen. An old steel wheel with thick spokes had been used for the front wheel.

This giant wheel barrow, which has an iron tractor wheel for its front wheel, is another unusual art object sitting near the entrance of Possum Kingdom State Park. Again, there is no information to indicate who created this. Photos by Eddie Lane and Norm Snyder.

"I don't know about the world's biggest, but that is one big wheelbarrow," said Eddie. "I know one other thing. I would not want to use that to carry any dirt in."

We wanted to look at it closer but another posted, keep-out sign was nailed onto a fence post. Norm shook his head and said, "You people in Texas do have a large way of doing things."

Eddie took several photos of the giant barrow and said, "The only reason I can see for that wheelbarrow is somebody wanted to practice their welding skills." That made sense to me. It was in a nice setting. Flashes of fall colors and milkweeds and blooming yellow broom weeds grew around it. It would have made a nice setting for an oil painting.

We left and drove to Possum Kingdom dam and looked at the stone bridge built about a mile down the river from the dam. This bridge was built by WPA (Works Progress Administration) workers during the Depression of the 1930s. The rocks were hand-cut from the local countryside and masons used them in a series of arches to form the bridge. Dr. T. Lindsay Baker has called it one of the top 100 historic sites in Texas. We used a photo of the bridge taken by Eddie for the back cover of my book, *Bridges Over the Brazos*.

As we looked at the bridge, a plane flew over us. Its engines made loud sounds that echoed for a long way down the curling Brazos River and through the surrounding hills. We left and drove on to Mineral Wells where we rented a motel room to be used for our base camp after we left Breckenridge.

We headed back toward Breckenridge. We got a call from Dan Strickland, a staff member of Bob Phillips' *Texas Country Reporter*. He had called us earlier after being told about our walk by my son-in-law, Brian Billeaudeaux. Strickland said Phillips wanted to do a story about the walk and could we meet them tomorrow in Palo Pinto. Of course we agreed. "Hey, we are going to be bigtime TV stars," said Norm.

"Maybe," said Eddie.

At any rate, it did kind of thrill me. During my days as a *Star-Telegram* columnist, I had watched Phillips' show regularly. He and I frequently had done stories on the same subject. I had always wanted to write a column about him but we had never been able to make connections. So, now, I was going to get to meet him.

We arrived back at Breckenridge. We checked in at our motel, ate an early dinner and retired to our rooms. I had gotten a boost, either from the walking or driving. But, I went to sleep not feeling nearly as homesick as I had earlier in the day.

Chapter Twenty-five

We walked through Palo Pinto
And then came Mineral Wells
A town famous for its waters
And, the old Baker Hotel.
Walk across Texas
With its wonderful sights.
Walk across Texas
With its beautiful nights.

We checked out of our motel in Breckenridge and headed east. We drove past used trucks for sale, stacks of pipe of all sizes, oil well pumps, and derricks. We drove about fifteen miles to reach our stations that would lead us into Palo Pinto. As usual, I had the first station.

When Eddie let me out, I felt hungry, generally a sure sign of a low blood sugar episode approaching. But, I knew I had eaten breakfast about an hour before and my mind began playing tricks on me as I reasoned, "If I ate an hour ago, then my blood sugar should not be low."

"Are you sure you are all right?" asked Eddie. He has developed a good sense of when my blood sugar may be falling. I assured him that I was and he said, "All right. I'll see you down the road."

I began walking in the rugged ranching country with hills and pastures filled with cedars, mesquites and live oaks. Fog and light rain hung over the landscape like a heavy curtain. I began walking up a rather long and steep hill. I found myself having trouble concentrating and my feet felt like they had air bags attached to them. I kept walking but my mind kept telling me, "Hey, Bunky, you need to stop and eat something."

When I finally reached the top of the hill, I did stop. I pulled a package of peanut butter crackers from my pack and crammed them into my mouth. I also had a package of an energy mix of raisins, nuts, and M&Ms that Norm had made. After the crackers, I stuffed that into my mouth. I still was having trouble getting my thoughts straight. So I emptied my pack onto the ground. I found the remnants of an energy bar and a candy bar. I ate them. Then I took a drink of water and just stood there, leaning on my hiking stick. Finally, after about ten minutes, my mind began to clear. I thought how dumb I had been to push myself when I knew that my blood sugar was low. But, after walking about another mile, I felt fine.

I looked to the side of the road at huge patches of milkweeds with white flowers blasting through the grayness. Sheets of bright fall colors, particularly those from sumac turning red, flashed brightly over the pasture-lands. I looked up at the sky and wondered about the pioneers who came over this land seeking treasures and happiness. I wondered how many of their offspring remained in the country and how many of them really cared about the land. I hoped there were lots of them.

I reached Eddie and we drove to Palo Pinto where Norm had walked. We ate lunch at the Palo Pinto Café. Eddie and Norm talked about seeing the remnants of old Highway 80, once a major artery taking people west in search of new lives. Eddie told about meeting a man named Jerry Robertson who lived at Metcalf Gap. "We need to go back and interview him," he said. "He's quite a character."

We decided to drive to Mineral Wells and stopped at the trailhead of Lake Mineral Wells State Park and Trailway. The start of the twenty-mile trailway that follows the bed of a former railroad line leading to Weatherford is in downtown Mineral Wells. I have walked the trailway several times and written several columns about it when I worked for the *Star-Telegram*. I have always enjoyed the trail.

We parked at the site and began looking for a map of the trail. The old vacant Baker Hotel, once a luxurious facility that offered rooms as well as health facilities peeked at us from the north. An old railroad car that is parked at the start of the trail fascinated Norm. "I've never seen a car like this before. It has seats and a toilet. I wonder what it was used for," he said.

As we looked at other things, David Owens of the Texas Parks and Wildlife Department arrived. We told him that we were planning to walk the trail within the next couple of days. "This is a part of a 450-mile walk we are making across Texas," said Norm. "Jon is going to write a book about our experiences."

Owens looked at me and said, "You'd better check with our park superintendent first. He can tell you if its legal for you to write anything about the trailway and whether it's libelous or not." I stared back at him. I could feel heat coming to my face. I could not believe he would even suggest that my writing about the trail might be libelous. I finally responded by saying, "That is the most stupid thing that I have ever heard of. I have written many stories about the trail, all of them quite complimentary. But, how could writing about a facility that has been built for the public become libelous, in any way." My voice had grown in intensity. Eddie interrupted me and said, "We appreciate your advice. We will see you later."

Both Norm and Eddie shook their heads about Owens' statement. We all talked about it and I finally settled down. We drove around Mineral Wells and looked at the old Baker Hotel and the Crazy Water Hotel. In our earlier talk with Dan Strickland he had said that Bob wanted to do the filming tomorrow and that they would like to have a camping scene for the film. However, we had discovered that Mineral Wells State Park was filled.

"I don't mind going to Lake Mineral Wells and see if they have a camping spot in the spill-over area," said Eddie. "If they do, then I'll camp there tonight and tomorrow so we'll have a camping spot for the filming."

"How about the weather forecast with the possibility of rain?" I asked.

"I think I can manage," said Eddie.

We agreed and he left us at a motel on the east side of Mineral Wells. Norm came to my room and we had a drink.

"What did you think of Dan, Dan, the Ranger man?" he asked.

I shook my head. "I think it's funny that we have walked nearly 400 miles and he is the first person to even offer a hassle to us," I said. "I don't know. Maybe he was just trying to be helpful."

After dinner, we returned to my room. We talked for while. Norm said, "I wonder what I should wear for the filming. Should I cut my own hair? Practice my 1000-yard stare? Maybe lose some weight?" he asked.

We both laughed. He retired to his room. I read some of my notes that I had taken during the walk. I remembered something Eddie had said this morning. "We are only about seventy miles from home," he said. I could not believe it.

Chapter Twenty-six

Bob Phillips heard about us
As we walked long and slow
He said, "I'm so impressed with you
I'm gonna put you on my show."
Walk across Texas
With its wonderful sights.
Walk across Texas
With its beautiful nights.

Eddie greeted us this morning with stories about the huge camping rigs he had seen at Lake Mineral Wells State Park. He said some of them must have cost $500,000 and had everything from central heat and air to television and elaborate sound systems. Despite their ambiance, he said he felt right at home in the $300 Highway Hilton.

We drove west to where we had ended our walk yesterday. We planned to walk to Mineral Wells today and possibly interview the man Eddie had met the day before. As we drove through Palo Pinto I recalled some historical information that Mel Rhodes, a pleasant person and editor of the *Mineral Wells Index,* had given me about the tiny town that is the county seat. It had once been known as Golconda. "No records are known detailing how the town Golconda was selected but a town by that name in India was the center of the ancient diamond industry and over the years the name has become associated with great wealth," read a historical report written by Bob Bellamy. "The district court met in the town of Golconda (it reads in the first twenty pages of county court records) [but]; mysteriously, [when] a meeting two weeks later was held in Palo Pinto, Golconda had disappeared and Palo Pinto used."

Another story in the report told about James Alvis Lynch, a wagon maker, who moved to this country in 1877. The family made a stop in their wagon in December of that year. They had two oxen pulling the wagon loaded with their belongings. Since there were no bridges, they had to ford the Brazos River. The day was hot and when they reached the other side, one of the oxen died from a heat stroke. Lynch and his sons began skinning the animal. "We can use that hide later on for shoes," the father said. Just as they finished their task, a Texas blue norther blew in and the other ox froze to death.

So life was tough in those days. As I looked across the ranchland, some of it choked by junipers and mesquite, I figured that trying to bring

Jon McConal, left, and Norm Snyder, right, talk to Jerry Johnston of Palo Pinto.
Johnston is a retired school superintendent. Photos by Eddie Lane and Norm Snyder.

cattle out of some of that would be as tough on riders and horses today
as what the Lynches had faced.

We stopped at Jerry Johnston's place west of Palo Pinto at a landmark known as Metcalf Gap. Johnston is a slender man and on this day
wore a red shirt and striped overalls. His dark hair had a dusting of gray
on the edges. He talked about being raised near the Brazos River in Knox
County and playing and walking along the river with his dog. After
receiving his high school diploma, he eventually earned his bachelor's and
master's degrees. "All I lacked were twelve hours for my doctorate. But,
I said when I got my master's that I was through and I was taking no
more courses," he said.

He became a schoolteacher and eventually served as a high school
principal at Millsap where he retired. "I also coached everything including
the one act play," he said. "I bought this place in February. You see that
gap behind me (a large, natural passageway between two mountains)? The
Indians used to come out of Oklahoma and come through that gap and
raid the ranchers and farmers in this area. Then they decided that they
could trade with the white man without raiding his property, so they set
up a trade station here. That's Metcalf Gap."

He called himself "just an old country boy." "I love living here with my
family and my dogs," he said. "Oh, yeah. I've got a granddaughter who
plays the fiddle and we go over to Mary's (a café in nearby Strawn) and

These falling down walls once housed a liquor store west of Palo Pinto. The walkers saw many such empty sites that once had been scenes of activity. Photos by Eddie Lane and Norm Snyder.

she really entertains the folks. Her name is Skye Hall and she won the grand champion fiddling title the last two years at Stamford."

We said our good-byes and drove to the remains of an old liquor store about a mile from Johnston's place. He said the woman who ran this used to keep a six pack of cold beer for him and when he got through teaching each day, he would stop to get it. "I would wait until her granddaughters got off the school bus and I would spend thirty minutes or so tutoring them," he said. I got out of the car and walked around the place where I had once bought liquor during my trips through this part of the country. The pungent smell of age seeped from the rocks and wreckage of the building. I leaned on my walking cane and realized that I could also smell the socks and shoes on all of us. I thought, "Maybe this trip has gone on long enough."

We drove down a gravel road to look at an old church at Springer Gap and Dodson Prairie. The church, painted white, sits on a hill and looks so pretty with its steeple, cross and green roof. I walked up to the building with stained glass windows and looked inside. An oilfield pump chugged in the background. The wind blew strongly, making the grass weave in and out like sinners did on Sundays when they heard the old invitation hymns to come on down and seek forgiveness for all of their misdeeds. I walked over a pathway made from Thurber brick. Grass blades punched up through the cracks around the bricks.

The walkers discovered this old church after driving down a gravel road that led to Dodson Prairie west of Palo Pinto. Services are still held at the church and nearboy is the Dodson Prairie Cemetery with this beautiful cross framed by cedar trees. Photos by Eddie Lane and Norm Snyder.

Nearby stood the Dodson Prairie Cemetery. We walked there and looked at some of the tombstones of families named Teichmann, Stanzel, and Kasper. One rather elaborate marker had a carving of a rose on each side of the name Holub. We also looked at markers for the Cashatts, Brothers, Nowaks, Ankenbauers, and a cross between rows of junipers. The cemetery is well kept and far off we could hear a bulldozer as it gouged brush from the land and pushed it into piles.

We rested on a bench and drank from our water bottles. "This is downright pleasant," said Eddie. I agreed and then looked at my watch. "We need to go to Palo Pinto, eat lunch, and meet Bob Phillips," I said. We walked back to the car and drove east to get ready for show time. One thing for certain, we smelled like we had walked a long way.

Phillips and his crew had not arrived at the Palo Pinto Café when we got there. Eddie and Norm sat on the porch and I walked over to the courthouse, a stately old building where I had covered several criminal trials when I worked as a reporter for the *Star-Telegram*. I walked up the stairs and looked into the district courtroom and thought about a trial I had covered in which a man had been charged with raping a nine-year-old girl. The late Sam Cleveland was district attorney and the late Billy Oxford was judge. What a pair they were.

The defendant had said he was crazy at the time of the offense and had based his defense on that premise. He had no attorney when first arrested and none eagerly stepped forward until two Dallas attorneys saw the story on television and had instantly felt sorry for the defendant. They had announced from Dallas that they would represent him free of charge.

The date for the trial had been set almost immediately. The two Dallas attorneys arrived as Judge Oxford convened the court. They were smiling and shaking hands with people. Judge Oxford asked Cleveland if he were ready to go to trial.

"I am your honor," boomed Cleveland in that voice of his that sounded like a shotgun being fired inside a shower stall.

Suddenly a look of apprehension came over the faces of the two Dallas lawyers. They began stammering that they had not had time to prepare their case and had not had time to even interview their client.

"But, you said on television, that you were ready to come down and represent this man and you insinuated that our legal system had mistreated him. Is that not true?" asked the judge in a commanding voice.

"Well, yes, but, your honor," one of the lawyers stammered.

"I asked you, 'Is that not true?'" thundered the judge.

The attorneys nodded their heads up and down in agreement, bending their faces toward the floor.

"Mr. Sam, are you ready to make your opening argument?" asked the judge.

"I am, your honor," bellowed Cleveland.

"Then proceed," said Oxford.

The Dallas attorneys said there was no way they could go to trial at this time. They needed at least four or five or six weeks in order to prepare their case.

"Then I am holding you in contempt of court," said the judge. "Sheriff Somerfeld, will you take these two gentlemen from Dallas to our county jail."

The two attorneys remained in jail until late in the afternoon. The temperature reached near 100 degrees. The jail had no air conditioning. When the two men finally got a friend to come and make their bail, they looked like two men who had been hauling hay all day long in their suits. Their fancy hairstyles had wilted. I had slipped down to the door leading outside when the men appeared swabbing with handkerchiefs at the perspiration that had drenched them. One of the men looked at me and said, "I'll tell you one thing about justice in this town, you had better not even get a parking ticket unless you have enough cash to pay your way out of jail."

I smiled as I remembered the scene and then walked back to the café that has an old looking clock sitting in front. A sign, surrounded by neon, read, "Time to eat," and the clock read nine-thirty. Eddie laughed and said, "Some place it's bound to be nine-thirty, so let's eat." While we waited for Phillips' crew, we chatted with Tommy and Tammy Roger who live in nearby Fortune Bend. He's tall and had his jeans stuffed into his boot tops. He talked about being raised on the Brazos River and how hard it was to judge the amount of water in the river's channel.

"Yes, and he has a boat and when we go to the river and it's low, I pull it," she said. She motioned with her hands. "He'll turn it on and we'll drive a few yards and get stuck again. I get out and start pulling. But, it's a lot of fun." They said goodbye just as Phillips' crew, led by Dan Strickland, arrived. We drove to a bridge north of town where Phillips met us. He has black hair with gray tingeing the edges. He's personable.

The film crew shot several takes of Phillips and me walking across the small bridge. Then Phillips spent about an hour and a half interviewing me. He asked about the people we had met and what, if anything, I had discovered about myself while walking this far. I laughed and said, "I discovered that I have become one of those being interviewed instead of the one doing the interviewing." Phillips finished his part and told me, "You are going to learn that there is much more to doing a television feature than there is for a newspaper. Regardless, it's been a pleasure meeting you and I wish you and your buddies the best of luck."

Bob Phillips of *Texas Country Reporter*, left, walks with Jon McConal near Palo Pinto. Phillips interviewed the trio for his television show. Photos by Eddie Lane and Norm Snyder.

He left and his crew spent another six hours filming us walking, going into an old store at Lone Oak, and then me walking into the campground at Lake Mineral Wells where Eddie and Norm had established a camping site. When I got there, they sat around a campfire and offered me a cup of coffee. Norm laughed and said off camera, "In real life, I'd be offering Jon a shot of Scotch."

Strickland also laughed as he finally turned off the monstrously large camera he had been lugging around. "We certainly appreciate your tolerance and patience. We'll get out of your hair now and you can have a real drink," he said. We shook hands and watched the taillights of their two vehicles being washed away by the darkness. We took out our bottles and poured three stiff drinks and sipped on them as we watched the moon trying to crawl its way through several wide strips of dark clouds. "Hey, it's all right being Jon McConal, a big time film star," I said. Eddie sipped his whiskey and replied, "Who's Jon McConal?" We all laughed and listened to an owl that had just begun its nightly prowl as it cooed, making what has to be one of the loneliest sounds in the world.

Chapter Twenty-seven

We liked Mineral Wells so much
We stayed an extra night.
We drank its mineral waters
And looked at other fine sights.
Walk across Texas
With its wonderful sights.
Walk across Texas
With its beautiful nights.

We made today's walk a short one. Eddie had informed us that we really did not lack many miles until we reached Granbury and since we wanted to accomplish that on October 31, it meant that we could either have several days of no walking at all, or walk shorter segments. We chose the latter.

Norm and I decided to walk the first five miles of the twenty-mile trail leading to Weatherford. We planned to meet Eddie at Garner, a small community that is about six miles from the trailhead. We wore sweatshirts and I had on a winter cap to cope with the brisk north wind that nipped at us as we moved down the trail. We saw some cattle grazing on new winter wheat fields. A couple of bicyclists waved as they sped past us. But, other than them and us, there was nobody else on the trail.

We reached Garner where Eddie and Mel Rhodes waited for us. Eddie talked about the huge number of raccoons that had been on the prowl around the camping area. "We needed a traffic cop to direct the raccoons going across the roads," he said. Mel asked us to pose for a photograph. "I brought you some information on the welcome sign that you asked about yesterday," he said. "It does have quite a history."

He made reference to a huge lighted Welcome sign that was erected on a hillside in 1922 near downtown Mineral Wells. D.W. Griffith, a noted producer and director of silent movies, saw the sign during a visit to Mineral Wells in 1929. It so inspired him that he went back to Hollywood and erected a huge lighted sign over a housing development called Hollywood Lane. Viewers frequently see this sign today in movies and television shows.

The lights in the Mineral Wells sign required constant care. They were replaced several times by other lights. The sign was turned off several times. Then it was moved from its first location east to Bald Mountain. Again, deterioration caused it to be shut down. Then a local radio station discovered the sign, cleaned, repainted, and restored the floodlights. It became the Mineral Wells Welcome sign again and beams out its message today.

"I was born about two blocks from the Baker Hotel," said Rhodes. "I grew up in and around Mineral Wells and remember the sign when it was on East Mountain and have been up to visit it where it sits now on Bald Mountain that has been renamed Welcome Mountain. It's quite a view from up there."

He said we should visit the Famous Water Company and the washing machine museum during our stay in Mineral Wells. He looked at the trail that would lead us to Weatherford tomorrow. "When they built this, all that remained of the rail service was an old engine and a few rickety cars," he said. "The tracks were rickety, too. The train could barely make five miles an hour when it ran over them. They turned it into this trail in the early 1990s."

He gestured at the nearby Garner Store and Café. "You knew that is where the domino game of 42 was invented, didn't you?" he asked. I did because I had once written a column about that. We listened to the wind rattle the leaves like dominoes being shuffled and decided to call it a day for our walking. We said goodbye to Mel and drove first to what may be the only washing machine museum in Texas or maybe the nation. It's located at the Fluff-N-Fold Laundromat in downtown Mineral Wells. It is well worth a stop.

Fred Nelson, former owner of the laundromat, started the museum when he bought an old piece of equipment at an antique sale. He had no idea what the machine that looked like a half barrel did until he opened a lid and saw an agitator. He realized that he had bought an antique washing machine. That was the beginning of the museum. An unusual thing about the facility is that customers wash and dry their clothing on modern machines positioned around the displays of the antiques.

A platform has been built to keep the old washing machines off the floor. They include a Thor electric washing machine made by Hurley Machine Company. It has a massive set of gears and I thought, "My gosh, I would have hated to have gotten caught in one of those." A warning on another early electric model read, "Grandma had to be very careful or she would find her hand going through the wringer." The museum has other aging items inside a glass case that include shoe stretchers, a Zippo cigarette lighter, castor oil, and a camera made out of a Budweiser beer can.

"We get a lot of people who come in only for a look at the antiques. They say they've never seen anything like it before," said Brianna Summerhill, laundromat attendant. We thanked her and drove to the Famous Water Company, the only mineral water company operating today in a city that once was famous for its mineral baths and mineral water. History says that a woman suffering from some form of dementia drank from one of the early mineral water wells and was cured. The well became known as the Crazy Woman's well. And, strange as it seems, Bob Bellamy wrote in a historical paper that the story might be true. "Modern analysis of the mineral water reveals traces of the rare earth element lithium, which is used extensively in modern medicine to treat a wide range of mental disorders," he said.

Today, Bill and Helen Arneson and Carol and Scott Elder own the water company. Bill Arneson met us and gave us a tour. He's a tall, friendly man with a great sense of humor. "This well is pretty much the one that built this town," he said. "We get claims that it helps arthritis and rheumatism. That's what it did 100 years ago and is still doing it today." We sipped free samples of the mineral water. It didn't taste that bad, really. "We ship the water everywhere like to Oklahoma and New York," he said. "People drink it once and they want to keep drinking it."

He showed us a long list of testimonials from people who have drunk the water. "I came from Europe to taste of Mineral Wells water, and well, it's great," wrote one. "The crazy water got me off my Previcet. It's been two months since I've taken any," said another. "I take one six ounce glass of crazy water at night and I don't get any asthma attacks during the night," said another.

We took one last sip and looked at the cement floors and steel tile ceilings and an old bar made from marble. I don't know about the water's curative powers but the Famous Water Company is a delightful place to visit.

We left and I told Eddie and Norm that I wanted to see if a steel boat that a man was building in his backyard was still there. I had written a column about the man several years ago. His dream had been to build this rather large boat and trailer it to Seattle where he and his wife planned to board the ship and sail it around the world. We drove through a residential neighborhood on the southeast part of town. We drove up a hill and I finally remembered the street where the man had lived. We turned down the street and drove about half a block and there the boat sat. It had never been completed and rust ate at the steel sides and deck. The house looked empty but we knocked anyway. Nobody came to the door.

We walked back and looked at the boat with its huge propellers and drive shafts that had never touched water. The wind kicked up the leaves, making rattling sounds around what had once been a man's dream. None of us said anything as we walked back to the car and drove back to the motel.

Chapter Twenty-eight

We breezed into Weatherford
A historic old town
We drove around the country
For a good look around.
Walk across Texas
With its wonderful sights.
Walk across Texas
With its beautiful nights.

I've always had adventuresome dreams. Last night's was no exception. I dreamed about the expanse of the Panhandle where we had walked and where we could gaze ahead and it was like looking into forever or some distant date. I dreamed I was there looking and the roads became blurred-out ribbons and the winds bent the grass and brought moans into the area.

I dreamed I was a reporter again and was looking for a telephone to call my story to the Fort Worth office. But, all I could see was this wide-open horizon with thin clouds that looked like fingers reaching down to caress me. I remembered my childhood days in West Texas and those furious sandstorms that blotted out the afternoon sun and blew thin sheets of dust and sand that settled on the furniture and floors of the houses.

I dreamed about the wind never ceasing and always echoing, sometimes in such powerful bursts like loud crescendos from a dramatic point in a symphony performance. The wind stayed constant, always there. And, even when it died, it still hammered the shadows in a dulled sound and depressed some people so much that they went crazy listening to that wind battering their houses and landscape.

In this dream, the wind hammered the landscape and me. But, the landscape that started out as a barren and misshapen place became smooth on the edges and vibrant colors came and then I realized I had forgotten about my story and getting it to the newspaper. I said to myself, "To hell with it. Look at the beauty of this place and listen to the power of the wind." Then the sun came up and there was a blaze of beauty and suddenly I knew there were more important things than writing this story that would be forgotten in ten days or less. And, then, I'm awake. I shook my head and I looked at the calendar. Only three more days were left on this trip.

Eddie picked Norm and me up and we drove to the halfway point of the remaining fifteen-mile route to Weatherford. Chickens ran across the road looking like they were chasing the last dash of fall colors. We saw a man on top of a roof, making repairs. We stopped and looked and listened to the repeated shots coming from his hammer. We stopped at Garner and let Norm out for his 5.6-mile section of walk. Then Eddie and I drove up the road. We passed fields with a bright sheen left by last night's dew on top of the new grain. We drove past cows licking and nuzzling new calves standing on tiptoes beside their mothers. We drove past two buckskin horses that had their heads plunged deeply inside a round bale of hay. We stopped, parked, and began our walk to the end of the trail in Weatherford.

I drank some orange juice and ate a package of peanut butter crackers. I also ate an apple as we walked past a beautiful patch of sunflowers with large yellow heads. We met two women riding bicycles. Eddie shouted at them, "I'd take your picture but my film is not slow enough." The women laughed and continued riding.

We saw some sumac with fall leaves so red they looked like flames from a fire. We passed a grain field that looked like it had green carpet layered on top of it. We heard the honking from geese flying overhead. I looked up at them and again was impressed with their majesty.

We crossed an old wooden bridge made out of railroad cross ties. We saw a flock of wild turkeys scatter across the trail in front of us. One stopped and turned its head for a direct look. Then it made that crazy turkey cry that goes, "Kerrrerryeah. Kerrerryeah. Kerrerrryead," and followed his buddies into the brush.

We stopped at a huge swarm of Monarch butterflies and watched as they fanned their wings, slamming into each other as they continued their great migration to Mexico. What a beautiful sight. We walked a short distance further and came to some wild flowers that looked like somebody had spilled purple paint onto them. Somebody later told me they might have been wine cups.

We passed some more bicyclists and Eddie repeated his earlier joke about taking their picture but his film was too slow. Then we could see the end of the trail. We kept walking and reached the benches provided at the end. Norm had not arrived so we sat down. We listened to the panting made by a man who had run a section of the trail. He sounded like a broken vacuum cleaner and kept saying, "Thank you, Jesus. Thank you."

Norm arrived and we loaded up and drove to the home of Stephanie Eidson, Eddie's daughter. She had agreed that we could stay at her house during our final nights. It sits on spacious acreage southwest of Weatherford. Two dogs, Isaac and Bear, recognized Eddie and licked his hands and nuzzled his legs in greeting. Stephanie, a registered nurse, was leaving for her job at Harris Hospital in Fort Worth.

"Make yourselves comfortable," she said. "I'm sure that dad will cook you a good meal. I will see you either tonight or in the morning."

We unloaded our gear and parked the Highway Hilton. Eddie got some of our gear from inside the tiny trailer and we carried it into the house. I went outside and walked around Stephanie's ranch. It is really nice. Cattle grazed the pastures and round bales of hay that had recently been cut and baled dotted the fields. I returned to the house. We all poured ourselves drinks and said little as Eddie cooked dinner. He grilled chicken, zucchini squash, potatoes, and corn on the cob—delicious.

"You know me. I am always cooking to keep our calories up," he said. "And, it helps if you aren't cooking on a Coleman."

After dinner, I called Jane. Her voice sounded so good. I asked her to put Cleo, our dog, on the phone. She held it up to the dog's ear and I said, "Hello, Cleo, your daddy is coming home." The dog didn't make a sound but Jane said she acted like she recognized my voice.

I went back outside and petted the dogs. I had learned that Isaac, a black Labrador, is sixteen. Bear is also ancient and has red spots. He is half lab and half Dalmatian. So he is called a Dalmatian with red spots. Both are friendly and love having the point behind their ears rubbed.

I returned to the house and found that I had been assigned the room that belongs to Stephanie's daughter, Marti, a senior at Baker University in Baldwin City, Kansas. She is going to school on a tennis scholarship. One of the original donors at the school was Abraham Lincoln. The room is brightly decorated. I had to take several teddy bears from my bed. As I crawled beneath the covers, I thought of how neat it was to be in a family home once again after some twenty-eight days on the road. I slept soundly.

Chapter Twenty-nine

We thought way back
To when this walking began.
Many were the times
When we thought it would never end.
Walk across Texas
With its wonderful sights.
Walk across Texas
With its beautiful nights.

Norm had gotten up early and had changed all of the clocks he could find to the new Daylight Savings Time. Stephanie, who had already left for work, later told us she had arrived an hour early. Barbara and Jane had called and said they would join us this morning and we would go to church. While we waited, we talked about our trip. We looked at a map of Texas and with our fingers traced the route starting at the Oklahoma border and followed it to Highway 180 and then east to Weatherford. We had done this repeatedly during the walk, tracing our progress. I wondered what Samantha, my eight-year-old granddaughter, would think about the walk and how many questions she would ask me about different things.

Eddie has a way of not looking exactly at you sometimes when he talks and makes a statement. His voice has a growling sound to it. He looked away from the map and said, "Boys, that is quite a distance. And, we're almost home."

We heard the dogs barking and saw that Jane and Barbara had arrived. We walked outside and greeted them warmly. I said, "It's nice to be around some women who have bathed and used some nice smelling perfume."

They both laughed. "What kind of women have you been around? Those that smell like wild hogs?" asked Barbara.

Norm and I climbed into the car with them and we drove to All Saints Episcopal Church. Father Scott Wilson is the priest and after the services he stood in the front door greeting people. When he got to Jane, he asked her where she was from. When she said Granbury, he asked if she were visiting somebody.

"Yes, him," she said, pointing at me.

"And, what are you doing here? Some kind of work?" he asked.

"No, I along with my friend Norm Snyder here, and one other friend, are making a 450-mile walk across Texas. We only lack twenty-eight miles from here," I said.

"Are you serious?" he asked.

Both Norm and I assured him we were.

He shook his head in disbelief and then wished us well. We left church and ate lunch at a restaurant on the town square that stretches around Weatherford's beautiful old courthouse. We drove around town before returning to Stephanie's.

As we said our good-byes, I told Jane, "Sweetheart, I'm glad this is almost over."

"So am I," she said.

Afterwards we decided that we would walk half of the remaining twenty-eight miles this afternoon. But, first we drove our route that would take us over Highway 51. After a few miles, Eddie said, "There is Comanche Peak." We all looked south and saw the famous Hood County landmark that looked like a giant melted chocolate bar. We passed some mares with new colts standing in a pasture. The mothers licked the colts' forelegs.

"You know how many rivers and creeks we have passed on this trip?" asked Eddie.

We didn't so he began listing them. "We crossed the Canadian once, the Red River twice, the Pease River twice and the Double Mountain Fork, Salt Fork, Clear Fork, and the Brazos, I think three times," he said. Then he began reciting a long list of creeks including Stroud and Ioni that we had also walked across.

We had reached the bridge just north of Granbury. We decided that since a group of people planned to meet us for the final three-mile walk into the city, the safest route would be from Thorp Spring into Granbury. But, we all had concerns about walking over the bridge. We talked about that and Eddie finally said, "We'll cross that bridge when we come to it."

His play on words sounded funny. So I exploded into laughter. Eddie joined me. Norm looked at us with concern. "I think you guys are losing it," he said.

Eddie stopped laughing long enough to ask, "Do you know why we haven't seen any dead armadillos?"

"Why?" asked Norm.

"Because there's no chickens to show them how to get to the other side of the road," he said.

I thought maybe Norm might be right. We were getting a little head weary. We headed back for Weatherford. Eddie let me out on Highway 51 just past Interstate 20 and I began my five-mile section of walking. I immediately noticed that not only was the traffic much heavier but the drivers also seemed more aggressive. Then somebody rolled down their window and shouted an obscenity at me. I kept walking. I walked another mile and another obscenity was yelled at me. Then a car almost stopped and made a wolf whistle. I thought of all of the miles we had walked across the Panhandle and the western regions of Texas and the only things we had heard were people shouting encouragement or stopping to see if we needed help.

When I joined Eddie and Norm they both said they had experienced the same thing. "A guy pulling a boat trailer made a swerve at me," said Eddie. "I nearly turned my ankle in trying to get out of his way." Norm said similar hostile acts had been directed at him. "I had to get off the shoulder of the highway four times," he said.

We turned around and headed back for Stephanie's. We talked about the hostile acts again. "Oh, it's just people reacting differently," said Eddie.

When we got to the house, we greeted Eric and Bear, then went into the house. Eddie had left the Texas map open on the dining room table. I looked again at our route. I realized then that not only was it hard to imagine we had walked that far, but it was hard to imagine how far we had come before anyone had hassled us.

Chapter Thirty

Eddie's daughter Stephanie
Said we'd played a long game
So she cooked us a meal
And toasted us with champagne.
Walk across Texas
With its wonderful sights.
Walk across Texas
With its beautiful nights.

I talked to Stephanie this morning before we left. We talked about her nursing career and her father. I asked her how she felt about him making this walk.

"I wasn't surprised at all. He's always been a free spirit. I tell my friends about him doing this and say, 'I think it's pretty good for a seventy-seven-year-old man to be able to walk that far.'" Then she told me that she planned to cook us a special meal tonight in celebration of us nearing completion of the walk. "We'll have some champagne, too," she said.

I told her that sounded good. Then we drove to where we had concluded our walk yesterday. We took our stations and began the final mileage. During my first mile, I passed a herd of llamas. A white dog that I had read was used as a guard, played in the middle of the herd. When I walked by the fence, he suddenly noticed my presence and stood still and almost at attention as he watched me walk by.

I saw some Shetland ponies standing in the shade of a big live oak. They looked so pleasant and I remembered one of my experiences with Shetlands when I was a youngster in West Texas. I had ridden my horse to a friend's house and when I returned I noticed one of our neighbors had his corrals full of Shetland colts. I rode to the pens and saw him putting a saddle on one of the animals. I asked what he was doing.

"Taking the edge off these ponies," he said. "They haven't been broke yet and I am just trying to get them used to having a saddle on them and maybe some weight." He looked at me and said, "You wanna ride them. They ought to be fun for somebody your size." The invitation sounded great. So I spent the next two hours riding the Shetland broncs. I did so well, the neighbor invited me back for the whole week.

I reached the car, drove down the highway and picked up Eddie. He said he had had an experience with a Beagle puppy. "He ran out and followed me. I told him to go home and he looked at me with those big eyes and looked so pitiful," said Eddie.

The wind had increased to thirty miles an hour by the time we reached Norm. The forecast called for high winds and temperatures in the lower sixties. As we listened to the radio announcer read the forecast, I thought about how important that piece of news had become to us during the walk.

We met Pete Kendall, feature writer for the *Hood County News,* about five miles north of Granbury. He had written about our excursion before we left. This was our first time to see him since then. He interviewed us and then took our photograph. One of his first questions was, "Are you all still friends?" He laughed as I hesitated and then answered, "I'll admit that I've discovered some of Norm's and Eddie's idiosyncrasies that have intrigued me," I said. When Kendall pressed me to list some of these I declined and said, "I'm sure that they feel the same way about me."

After our walk, we still had most of the afternoon left. So we drove to Millsap where I thought the character Buster Brown, a man who stood a little more than three feet tall, had lived. The Buster Brown I remembered had been hired during the 1930s to go across the country promoting Buster Brown shoes. His dog Tige had accompanied him.

We stopped at the Millsap City Hall. Nobody there remembered him. We talked to a postal clerk named Sheryl Hearn. She had a history book of the area but no mention was made of a Buster Brown. She suggested I call the postmaster. I did. She said her name was JoAnn and she had been born there and at first she could not remember a Buster Brown. Then she said, "Oh, yes, I remember Buster Brown. He was a doctor," she said. I told her that was not the man I had been thinking about. "Well, I know you," she said. "I bought one of your bridges books. I wished you had interviewed me before you wrote it. You know that bridge on the cover . . . the old Tin Top Bridge. When they completed that bridge, my daddy drove his team and a wagon across it. They watched and when he made it across, they said, 'It must be okay.'"

We headed back for Weatherford on the old Millsap Highway. We passed four buffalo grazing on a coastal bermuda grass field. One of the buffalo had a calf. They made a peaceful scene. We stopped for a closer look and possible photograph. The wind had increased and grown colder. Of course, the buffalo with their massive coats could have cared less.

"They are magnificent animals," said Norm.

We stopped at the *Weatherford Democrat* where we were interviewed and had our photograph taken. We returned to Stephanie's house. Inside, the smells of good home cooking greeted us. "We're going to have pork loin, grilled potatoes, green beans, and banana pudding," she said.

While we sipped our drinks, Mark and Sarah Eidson, former in-laws of Stephanie who live on the ranch adjoining her, arrived to join the celebration for the completion of the walk. They both expressed surprise over what we were about to accomplish. We shared our experiences and then we ate. The food was delicious.

"This is better than what you've been eating out over the campfire, isn't it?" asked Sarah.

Eddie frowned and pointed at himself. "Watch what you say. I've been the cook," he said.

We all laughed and Stephanie opened the champagne. She filled our glasses and I said, "Here's to three guys who are about to finish a 450-mile walk across Texas." We all drank and somebody shouted, "Hear. Hear. Hear."

I was glad that the end was so close.

Chapter Thirty-one

When we reached Granbury
People made a loud cheer
They said "You old codgers made it.
You're welcome back here."
Walk across Texas
With its wonderful sights.
Walk across Texas
With its beautiful nights.

I went to bed feeling a scratchiness in my throat, and my nose had begun running. I took some aspirin and echinacea tablets that are supposed to increase the body's immune functions. I woke up at four A.M. My throat had gotten so bad I could barely swallow. So much for the echinacea. I took two more aspirin.

When I got up at six A.M., I really did not feel very good. I thought, "If today were not the big day, I certainly would stay at home and in bed." Aw, what the hell. I knew that I had things I had to do . . . walk the final three miles of our 450-mile trek.

I walked down the hall. I could smell coffee brewing. Norm looked up from his computer and said that the weather today would be in the upper sixties with strong north winds. We drank coffee and ate breakfast. We packed and carried our gear to the car. Bear and Isaac sat watching us. Eddie petted them and said, "You dogs make a pretty sight. The only thing that can beat this is to be sitting around a campfire watching the sun come up."

We climbed into the car and headed for Thorp Spring. This being the last day, I was surprised that none of us said anything reflective or philosophical. But, as I thought back, this really had not been much of a philosophical group. I remembered a question Pete Kendall had asked yesterday. "After a day of walking, and you were sitting around the campfire, what did you talk about?" We all had looked at each other and I had said, "Duh."

As we drove, Eddie said, "I've learned one thing from this trip. It was the Double Mountain Fork and not the Salt Fork that put that salt into the Brazos." I thought of all of the people we had met. I asked myself if I would attempt such a walk again.

I thought of the strings of red, blue, and black clouds, looking almost like shredded ribbons in those West Texas skies and the absolutely stunning beauty of them. I thought about that powerful wind smashing into our faces and blowing our hats off and bending those skinny stems of gramma grass almost to the ground and making the tree limbs bend in and out like dancers doing fancy steps to some tango. I thought of the blisters and the back pain and the urge calling to us every morning to get up and go, and stand in line for the sun to come up and be participants in this part of Texas and its rich life and growth. I thought of those and said to myself, "Yeah, I would do it again."

And, really, at age sixty-nine, I did not feel that I had pushed myself too hard physically. Mentally, maybe. I thought of all of those days when I wanted Jane to talk to and when I wanted to feel her lying beside me in my bed and when I had thought, "This is too much to take on." Feeling that and then hearing Jane say, "Aw, sweetheart, you can do it. You must do it."

Norm interrupted my thoughts. "The weather report for Perrryton this morning is winds out of the northeast at seventeen miles an hour with a wind chill factor at eighteen degrees," he said. "Oh, yeah, they are expecting possible sleet, too."

I rolled my tongue and sucked on my sore throat tablet. I looked at my notebook. I realized that I had taken something like 250 pages of notes. I smiled as I thought, "There's got to be a book in there somewhere." I looked across the pasture and saw crows sitting in some trees. I thought of their cries that I have always loved. Some people claim there's no melody in the crow's staccato blasts. But, to me, they break the shadows where loneliness abounds, shattering them with bold and loud cries like the crow is saying, "Here I am. Here I am. You're not the only one out here."

As we neared Thorp Spring, I felt a funny feeling come to my stomach like I feel sometimes before I make a speech. We passed some cattle eating hay, getting their bellies full as a protection against the coming blast of winter.

We arrived at 11:15 A.M. We had told people that we would begin the final three miles into Granbury at noon. Nobody was there yet but about fifteen minutes later, cars began arriving. Ian Moore was one of the first. He came over and shook my hand. "Remember seeing me on the city trail when you were training?" he asked. I did.

Jane and Barbara arrived. They had made sandwiches and brought carrots and celery sticks and bottled water. We ate and waited. Finally, at 12:15, I counted about twenty-five people. I decided that we should hit the road.

"All right, everybody, let's walk into Granbury," I shouted.

A policeman turned on his siren and flashing red lights and led us across the bridge. We headed up a hill and I chatted with people from the Hood County Habitat for Humanity chapter and other brave souls. The wind bit into us but nobody complained.

We reached the city limits and turned south toward the city hall. The line streamed out behind me. I looked and could see the courthouse steeple. I reached into my pocket for another aspirin. I swallowed it and kept walking.

Jon McConal, Norm Synder, and Eddie Lane lead a group of Granbury residents who walked the last three miles with them. Photos by *Mineral Wells Index* and *Hood County News*.

We reached the city trail over which I had walked many, many times in preparing for all of this. We turned onto it and followed it the rest of the way to the city hall. Mayor David Southern stood there awaiting us along with several other people. When we reached the platform, a loud cheer erupted from everyone. Eddie, Norm, and I held up our hands.

The mayor shook our hands and then said, "Jon McConal, you have done many things to bring good publicity to Granbury. But, I will have to say, you have outdone yourself with this walk across Texas."

We stayed for several minutes, shaking hands and telling about our experiences. Finally, I turned to Jane and said, "I'm ready to go home." She leaned in close to me and whispered, "Are you sure, you don't want to walk." Then she grabbed my hand and led me to the car, the end to what had been a wonderful experience.

The End

Epilogue

One question that has been repeatedly asked of the three of us since we completed our walk is, "Are you guys still friends? How did the walk affect your relationship?"

To answer the question simply, yes, we still are friends. Eddie and I have maintained our relationship of seeing each other about once a week and talking several times over the telephone. And, we are planning to take an extended camping trip to Big Bend National Park.

Norm and I have also maintained our relationship. We see each other Sundays at church and also once a week when we meet to work as volunteers helping construct houses for the Hood County Habitat for Humanity chapter. Eddie and Norm have talked to each other several times since the trip and there has been no erosion of their relationship.

Finally, we all appeared together to make a presentation about the walk to a social club in Granbury. We each took ten minutes to relate our experiences and when we finished, we all smiled during the applause.

Maybe Norm said it best in his summary of the trip. He wrote:

"We got along. I think we all learned what things were best left unsaid and for the most part, left them unsaid. We adjusted to each other's idiosyncrasies. For instance, Jon is fairly liberal in his politics and I am conservative in many areas, as is Eddie. We made a rule early on that we wouldn't discuss politics and we pretty well followed that rule.

"Jon and I are both churchgoers. Eddie is not. When the opportunity was presented, Jon and I could go to church and Eddie would find something else to do. He claimed it was to protect us from lightning strikes, but I told him that God doesn't miss.

"The fact that each one of us has a sense of humor made things immeasurably easier. Jon can be wry, and Eddie ribald. I'm probably somewhere in between.

"The bottom line is, would I do it again? Absolutely. We made it through the expedition with a few bruised egos but no casualties. Knowing what to expect and how to avoid some of the irritants would make the next project easier. But, I certainly would do it again."

So would Eddie and I.

Interviews

Scott, Belinda, Groom

Shadle, Brad, Clarendon

Snyder, Barbara, Granbury

Southern, David, Granbury

Strickland, Dan, Fort Worth

Suitor, Terri, Perryton

Summerhill, Brianna, Mineral Wells

Taylor, Andi, Spur

Thomas, Rosemary, Abilene

Tipps, Marian, Hamlin

Todd, Howard, Albany

Treull, Don, Breckenridge

Turner, Dan, Turkey

Wilson, Scott, Weatherford

WORKS CONSULTED

T. Lindsay Baker, *Ghost Towns of Texas*, University of Oklahoma Press, 1986.

T. Lindsay Baker, *More Ghost Towns of Texas*, University of Oklahoma Press, 2003.

J. Frank Dobie, *Tales of Old-Time Texas*, Little, Brown & Company, 1955.

Evetts Haley, *Charles Goodnight: Cowman and Plainsman*, University of Oklahoma Press, 1949.

William Kemsley, *Whole Hikers Handbook*, Wm. Morrow & Co., New York, 1979.

Jon McConal, *Bridges Over the Brazos*, TCU Press, 2005.

John Wesley Powell, *Down the Colorado: Diary of the First Trip Through the Grand Canyon*, Promontory Press, 1969.

Theodore Roosevelt, *Outdoor Pastimes of an American Hunter*, 1918.

Texas Almanac, Dallas Morning News, 2001.

Wheatheart of the Plains: An Early History of Ochiltree County, Ochiltree County Historical Survey Committee, 1969.

NEWSPAPERS CONSULTED

Breckenridge American, July, 2004.

Clarendon Chronicle, October, 2006.

Fort Worth Star-Telegram, September, 1982.

Miami Chief, October 10, 2006.

Mineral Wells Index, October, 2000.

Palo Pinto County Star, 1927.

Texas Spur, July, 2004.

San Antonio Express, 1892.

Weatherford Democrat, October, 2006.

Western Observer, October, 2006.

OTHER SOURCES

Handbook of Texas Online, http://www.tshaonline.org

INDEX

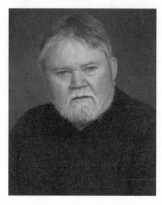

About the Author

Jon McConal, retired columnist for the *Fort Worth Star-Telegram*, won some forty-five writing awards, including being named top writer in Texas by the Texas Headliner Association during his forty years at the newspaper. McConal, a West Texas native, attended high school in Glen Rose and received his BA degree from Sam Houston State University and his MA from North Texas State University. He has three other books in print, including *Bridges over the Brazos*, (2005, TCU Press). He lives in Granbury with his wife, Jane.

ISBN 978-0-87565-363-1

5 1 9 9 5

9 780875 653631

A Walk Across Texas
ISBN 978-0-87565-363-1
Paper. $19.95